# Economics in the Bible

Kunsoo Paul Choi, Ph.D.

Parson's Porch Books

*Economics in the Bible*

ISBN: Softcover 979-8-89532-040-2



**Parson's Porch Books** is an imprint of Parson's Porch & Company (PP&C) in Cleveland, Tennessee. PP&C is a self-funded charity which earns money by publishing books of noted authors, representing all genres. Its face and voice is **David Russell Tullock** (dtullock@parsonsporch.com).

Parson's Porch & Company *turns books into bread & milk* by sharing its profits with the poor.

www.parsonsporch.com

# *Economics in the Bible*

# Contents

## PART III
## THE ECONOMY OF EVANGELISM



## PART IV
## CHRISTIAN ECONOMIC ETHICS

# Preface

Many people think that there is no or mere connection between economics and the Bible. When people hear that I majored in economics and biblical studies, they wonder why I studied the two quite different fields. Then, they guess that I just gave up what I previously studied (economics) to become a pastor. However, I think that the Bible teaches a lot about economics, which I define the study of decision making by economic agents – an individual, a firm, a market, or a government – in everyday life. Microeconomics is the study of an individual's decision making for him/her and his/her household to maximize utility (that is, satisfaction) and a firm's decision making to maximize its profit. Macroeconomics is the study of a government's decision making for a country as a whole under various situations of employment/unemployment, inflation, business cycles, growth, etc.

When we say about an economy, it generally means a situation or a status of a country in terms of employment/unemployment, inflation, gross domestic product (GDP) or consumption, exports/imports, and/or national budget/debts or of a household in its budget and/or consumption. However, in the New Testament, the Greek word, "*oikonomia*," which corresponds to the English word, "economy," is used more about (managing or governing) activity rather than a situation or a status. Its meanings in the New Testament include "stewardship or the management of the household" (Luke 16:2-4); "mission or dispensation (of spreading the gospel)" (1 Cor. 9:17); and God's plan or dispensation of human salvation" (Eph. 1:10). I believe that God wants his people to be saved not only spiritually but also materially. By "material salvation," I mean that God's people can also be saved materially in this world by learning economics of God – learning how to manage their time, money, and life according to the will of God and his instructions.

Although Paul in the New Testament limits the economy of God to his saving plan or dispensation, God's economy in the Bible includes his various governing or decision-making activities for the people in his household. God's economy starts with his blessing of human beings whom he had created according to his image and his likeness in

Genesis 1:28: "Be fruitful, multiply, and fill the earth." God's governing or economic activities in the Old Testament are to manage his household well and thus make the people in his household prosper. God's governing or economic activities should be done by the government in today's society. God's people, following God's example and instructions, are supposed to manage their households. God's economy can be expanded to more people and more nations though the mission of the church.

As a person who teaches economics, I want to connect my knowledge in economics with my understanding of the Bible and God's instructions. So, I will keep trying to find a way to let people know the sound economics of God that they can find in the Bible and apply its principles to their daily living accordingly. The Revised Standard Version (RSV) is primarily used unless I specify different versions for this book.

# Chapter One

# What is The Economy in the Bible?

## General Definitions of an Economy

An "economy" generally means a country's situation in terms of production and/or consumption of goods and services, employment or unemployment, inflation, economic growth, or the standard of living, etc. An economy may also be defined as "an activity of production, consumption, distribution, or trade of goods and services by different agents such as a household, a firm, or a government," or "the wealth and resources of a country or region, especially in terms of production and consumption of goods and services," or "careful management of available resources." A household economy is thus the wealth of a household or careful management of available and scarce resources for a household. A nation's economy is the wealth and resources of a country in terms of production and consumption or in connection with inflation, unemployment, gross domestic product (GDP), and economic growth. So, our understanding of an economy in economics textbooks is more likely a situation or a status of wealth and resources for a household or a country.

## Etymology of an Economy

The word economy (經濟, jingji) in Chinese is an abbreviation of '經世濟民'(jingshijimin), '經國濟世' (jingguojishi), or '經國濟民' (jingguojimin), said to be originated either from 書經 (Shujing, the Book of Documents), one of the Five Classics of ancient Chinese literature, or from 莊子(Zhuangzi or Chuang Tzu), which means that the government manages or governs the nation's general (including political, economic, and social) affairs and issues well and thus saves its people and makes them better off or prosper. This Chinese word, 經濟 (jingji), with its meaning, has been widely used in Asian countries – especially in China, Korea, and Japan – and includes not only the areas of economy but also the areas of politics and administration. That is, it is about a government's general activities, plans, or ways of governing its country and making its people prosper.

The Greek word, "*oikonomia* (οἰκονομία)," corresponds to the English word, "economy." The word, "*oikonomia*," is a compound word of "*oikos*" (= house) and "*nomia*" (= management). So, its original meaning is the management of a house or a household. The word, "*oikonomos* (οἰκονόμος)," is a manager of a household.

## Occurrences in the New Testament

The word '*oikonomia*' occurs nine times in the New Testament – three times in the Gospel of Luke (16:2, 3, 4), one time in 1 Corinthians (9:17), three times in Ephesians (1:10, 3:2, 9), one time in Colossians (1:25), and one time in 1 Timothy (1:4).

Jesus in Luke 16:2-4 says: "2And he (a rich man) called him (a steward)
and said to him, 'What is this that I hear about you? Turn in the
account of your <u>stewardship</u>, for you can no longer be steward.' 3And
the steward said to himself, 'What shall I do, since my master is taking
the <u>stewardship</u> away from me? I am not strong enough to dig, and I
am ashamed to beg. 4I have decided what to do, so that people may
receive me into their houses when I am put out of the stewardship.'"

Paul in Ephesians 1:9-10: "9For he (= God) has made known to us in
all wisdom and insight the mystery of his will, according to his purpose
which he set forth in Christ 10as a <u>plan</u> for the fullness of time, to unite
all things in him, things in heaven and things on earth."; in Ephesians
3:2 and 9: "2- assuming that you have heard of the <u>stewardship</u> of
God's grace that was given to me for you, …9and to make all men see
what is the <u>plan</u> of the mystery hidden for ages in God who created all
things."; in Colossians 1:25: "… of which I became a minister
according to the divine <u>office</u> which was given to me for you, to make

the word of God fully known, …"; and in 1 Timothy 1:4: "… nor to occupy themselves with myths and endless genealogies which promote speculations rather than the divine training (stewardship or order) that is in faith;"

## Meanings of *Oikonomia* in the New Testament

First, *oikonomia* means "stewardship or the management of a household" in the New Testament (Luke 16:1-4). The dishonest steward summoned each one of his master's debtors and reduced each debtor's debt on his or her bill. Later, the master knew what the dishonest steward had done and commended him for his shrewdness (Luke 16:8). However, it does not mean that the dishonest steward did the right thing but that he could find a way to survive in this world. Each one of us is a steward of God and what we do in this world is stewardship for God. As a steward of God, we should be honest and faithful.

Second, *oikonomia* means "mission or dispensation of (spreading or preaching) the gospel" (1 Corinthians 9:17; Ephesians 3:2; Colossians 1:25). Paul in 1 Corinthians 9:17-18 calls his mission or commission of spreading the gospel '*oikonomia.*' Paul in Ephesians 3:2 calls his mission to preach the good news to the Gentiles, including the people in Ephesus, "the stewardship (or commission, NRSV) of God's grace" that was given to him for the Gentiles. Paul regards his mission or stewardship (of spreading the gospel to the Gentiles) as "God's grace and gift." Paul in Colossians 1:25 speaks of his apostleship (of spreading the good news to the Gentiles) and regards it as "the divine office" that was given to him. The word apostle means 'the one who is sent' and every time Paul mentions his apostleship, he reminds of his duty/mission of spreading the gospel to the Gentiles. Paul uses the word, *oikonomia* (economy), in defining his mission or commission of spreading the gospel to the Gentiles, believing that his mission of spreading the good news is to bring people to God for them to be saved.

Third, in our relationship with God, *oikonomia* means God's plan or dispensation (of human salvation) (Ephesians 1:9-10, 3:2 & 9; 1 Timothy 1:4). Paul in Ephesians 1:9-10 and 3:9 uses *oikonomia* in connection with God, meaning God's saving plan of his people through Jesus Christ, which was hidden for a long time but is now revealed as the opportune time came. The "stewardship" of God's grace in Ephesians 3:2 can also be interpreted as God's salvation plan of his grace about which Paul was commissioned to preach. Paul in 1 Timothy 1:3-4 also uses *oikonomia* in connection with God, meaning the divine training (or plan, stewardship or order) in faith. Paul interprets or understands God's economy as his saving act or plan (or dispensation) of his people – believers/Christians – in his opportune time.

## General Definitions of Economics

Like an economy, there are various ways of defining economics: "the study of economic behaviors of different units such as a household, a firm, a market or an industry, a government, or a nation as a whole"; or "the study of how society chooses to allocate its scarce resources to the production of goods and services to satisfy unlimited wants"; or "the study of the choices people make to attain their goals, given their scarce resources." When we study economics, we study an economy of a household – its consumption behavior and goal to see how a household can manage its economy optimally; an economy of a firm – its production behavior and goal to see how a business can manage its business optimally; and an economy of a country – its aggregate supply and demand, economic growth, economic policies to see how the government can resolve economic issues such as inflation and unemployment and attain stable economic growth.

Economics usually consists of microeconomics and macroeconomics. Microeconomics is the study of how households and firms make choices, how they interact in markets, and how the government attempts to influence their choices; or the study of decision making by a single individual, household, firm, industry, or level of government. Macroeconomics is the study of the economy as a whole, including topics such as inflation, unemployment, and economic growth; or the study of decision making for the economy as a whole. I personally define economics as "the study of decision making" for a household, a firm, a market or an industry, or a government (Microeconomics) and for a country as a whole (Macroeconomics).

## Economics in the Bible

We observed that the word, economy (*oikonomia*) is used for three different meanings: 1. management or stewardship of a household; 2. mission, commission, duty, or office (of preaching or spreading the gospel) of Paul as an apostle; and 3. a plan or dispensation (of human salvation) of God. A literal translation of the word, economy (*oikonomia*), "management of a household" can represent all these different translations.

Paul performs the act of stewardship that 'was given to him for the Gentiles' (Eph. 3:2; Col. 1:25). That is, Paul manages the household of God by preaching or spreading the gospel (1Cor. 9:17; Eph. 3:2; Col. 1:25) to expand the business of God's household to the Gentiles (other nations and people). God manages His own household by making His plan (of saving people) known to His people (Eph. 1:10, 3:2, 9; 1Tim. 1:4) for the fullness of time.

So, what is economics in the Bible? Economics within the New Testament can be defined as the study of stewardship or management of an individual household, stewardship or management of God for His own household (kingdom of God), and Paul's and all Christians' stewardship of expanding God's household (kingdom of God) to other nations and people by spreading the gospel. We may call the study of stewardship or management of an individual household the microeconomic perspective; the study of stewardship of God for His own household (kingdom of God) the macroeconomic perspective; and the study of Paul's and all Christians' stewardship of expanding God's household (kingdom of God) to other nations and people the international economic perspective. As economics in general is about decision making, so economics in the Bible is about decision making for the household of God (macroeconomic aspects), for each individual household (microeconomic aspects), for the expansion of God's household (international economic aspects), and each individual's conduct (economic ethical aspects).

**Plan of This Book**

Part I of this book discusses the economy of God, which is the macroeconomic perspective and deals with macroeconomic topics. Paul mainly focuses on God's saving plan or act when he refers to "the economy of God" (ἡ οἰκονομία τοῦ Θεοῦ) in the New Testament as it is the most important and imminent matter for those who were lost by the grace of God. However, the economy of God includes not only his saving plan or act of human beings but also His various governing activities for His people as we can find in the Old Testament and Jesus' proclamation in the books of Gospels, especially in John. So, in Part I, we will study God's various governing activities and instructions on some macroeconomic topics, including daily food, land, loans, tithes/taxes, wealth, poverty, and others.

Part II deals with the economy of an individual household, which is the microeconomic perspective and deals with microeconomic topics. An individual household is the smallest unit of the household of God. Each individual of a household is a manager or steward who makes decision to manage a household that is entrusted to him/her by God. So, in Part II, we will study each individual's various managing and governing activities for his/her household and decision making on some microeconomic issues, including talent or money, labor and other resources.

Part III examines the economy of evangelism or the economy of the church as a whole, which is the international economic perspective. Luke in the Book of Acts describes Paul's experience of encountering with Jesus who appeared to him in the form of light on his way to Damascus (Acts 9:3-19, 22:6-16, 26:9-23). In Acts 26:15-18, Jesus tells Paul: "[15]… I am Jesus whom you are persecuting. [16]But rise and stand upon your feet; for I have appeared to you for this purpose, to appoint you to serve and bear witness to the things in which you have seen me and to those in which I will appear to you, [17]delivering you from the people and from the Gentiles – to whom I send you [18]to open their eyes, that they may turn from darkness to light and from the power of Satan to God, that they may receive forgiveness of sins and a place among those who are sanctified by faith in me." Paul in Galatians in 1:15-16 describes this experience in his own words: "[15]But when he (=

God) who had set me apart before I was born, and had called me through his grace, [16]was pleased to reveal his Son (= Jesus Christ) to me, in order that I might preach him among the Gentiles." Paul strongly claims his apostleship (from the Greek word, ἀποστέλλω, send out) as he regards it very seriously and it was disputed and opposed by Jewish Christians. To Paul, his apostleship is not authority but duty or commission, which was given to him by God, to preach the gospel to the Gentiles.

Paul's economy (mission, commission, duty, or office), which was given to him, is any Christian's economy as he/she belongs to Christ and is called to be a witness of Jesus Christ (Acts 1:8). Paul's economy is also the economy of the church as a whole that is the body of Christ who had come to us to preach the Kingdom of God and let us fully know God's salvation plan at his opportune time. The purpose or mission of the church is to preach or spread the gospel to many nations. By doing so, the economy of God is expanded to many nations and people and fully known to them (Matthew 28:19-20). So, in Part III, we will study the economy of evangelism, which is our mission of expanding the economy of God.

Part IV investigates Christians' economic ethics in the Bible. Each Christian belongs to a family or a household, a church, a company, a community, and a nation. How should each Christian's economic ethical conduct be as a member of each different unit? So, in Part IV, we will discuss Christians' economic ethics that we can find in the Bible.

# PART I

# THE ECONOMY OF GOD: MACROECONOMC ASPECTS

## Chapter Two

# What is the Economy of God?

### The Economy of God

Paul interprets or understands God's economy as God's saving act or plan (or dispensation) of his people – believers/Christians – in his opportune time (Ephesians 1:9-10, 3:2 & 9). God's economy is his saving act or plan of his people not only spiritually in God's kingdom but also materially in this world. The economy of God includes his saving plan or act of his people as well as his various governing activities for his people as we can find in the Old Testament and Jesus' proclamation in the Books of Gospels, especially in John. Our study of economics is about decision making for an individual as well as for a nation as a whole to maximize our satisfaction while we live in this world. Our study of God's economics is to know God's and his people's decision making to maximize their satisfaction or happiness in the household of God.

### God Blesses His Household

God's economy is found initially in Genesis 1:26-28: "[26]Then God said, 'Let us make man in our image, after our likeness; and let them have dominion over the fish of the sea, and over the birds of the air, and over the cattle, and over all the earth.' [27]So God created man in His own image, in the image of God He created him; male and female He created them. [28]And God blessed them, 'Be fruitful and multiply, and fill the earth and subdue it; and have dominion over the fish of the sea and over the birds of the air and over every living thing that moves upon the earth.'" God created man in their (=triune God's) image and in their likeness. The phrase, "in their image, in their likeness" Genesis 1:26-27), does not mean that man was created according to God's appearance but according to God's character and disposition. Man was given personality that made him think, feel, will and judge. Man was given conscience, morals and ethics. So, when he did something against God, he felt guilty. God's goodness, faithfulness, and righteousness were also given to the man. God's Spirit was given to the human couple so that they could worship God in spirit and in truth. God blessed human beings – Adam and Eve – that he created and wanted them to be fruitful (prosper), multiply (increase in number), and fill the earth and subdue it. What God wanted when He created the human couple, they who were in God's image would be fruitful, increase in number and fill the earth as God's ambassadors. The birds of the air, the fish of the sea, and animals and plants on the earth were all created to be ruled over by people. The purpose of God's creation of man was to rule over the fish of the sea and the birds of the air, over the livestock, over all the earth, and over all the creatures that move along the ground.

**Adam & Eve**

**in the Garden of Eden**

**God's First Household on the Earth**

However, as Adam and Eve fell, they lost most of their power to rule over the birds of the air, the fish of the sea, and the animals and plants on the earth as well as their eternal life. Human lifespan was reduced to less than 1,000 years from eternity (Genesis 5). Later, as human sins and trespasses became widespread on the earth, the human life was again reduced to 120 years (Genesis 6). Even after Adam and Eve fell, God's economy (management of his household) continued. God saved Noah and his family from the great flood (Genesis 6-8). God restored his blessings (for Adam and Eve) in Genesis 1:28 for Noah and his family in Genesis 9:1-3 and 7. Genesis 9:1-3 states: "[1]And God blessed Noah and his sons, and said to them, 'Be fruitful and multiply, and fill the earth. [2]The fear of you and the dread of you shall be upon every beast of the earth, and upon every bird of the air, upon everything that creeps on the ground and all the fish of the sea; into your hand they are delivered. [3]Every moving thing that lives shall be food for you; and as I gave you green plants, I give you everything.'" Then, God repeats his blessings upon Noah and his family one more time in Genesis 9:7: "And you, be fruitful and multiply, bring forth abundantly on the earth and multiply in it." We can see the goal of the economy of God is to let human beings that were created according to God's image and likeness "be fruitful, multiply, and fill the earth and subdue it" from the very beginning. Has the goal of the economy of God been changed? God wants his household, Christians, to be fruitful, multiply, and fill the earth.

God in Genesis 12:1-3 called Abram and told him: "[1]Now the LORD said to Abram, 'Go from your country and your kindred and your father's house to the land that I will show you. [2]And I will make of you a great nation, and I will bless you, and make your name great, so that you will be a blessing. [3]I will bless those who bless you, and him who curses you I will curse; and by you all the families of the earth shall bless themselves." Why did God call and select Abraham as a member of his household? God probably foresaw his genuine mind and faith. God promised to give Abraham and his descendants three things – land (Canaan), nations, and blessings. God continued to appear Abraham whenever he began to doubt God's promises to reconfirm him that his promises would be fulfilled for sure.

God blessed Abraham's son Isaac, Isaac's son Jacob, Jacob's sons Joseph and Judah. God did not forget the Israelites although they had lived a slavery life in Egypt for 430 years. God saved the Israelites from the hand of the Egyptians and lead them through Moses and then Joshua to the land of Canaan, "a land flowing with milk and honey" (Exodus 3:8, 17, 13:5, 33:3; Lev. 20:24; Deut. 6:3, 11:9, 26:9, 15, 27:3, 31:20; Joshua 5:6), the land that God had shown Abraham first. God's blessings continued throughout the history of the Israelites even when they turned away from God. God had been patient and waited until they returned to him. When the Israelites returned to him, his blessings were restored. God's blessings – an act of God's management of his household – reached its highlight when he had sent his only begotten Son, Jesus Christ, to the world and let him die on the cross.

### God Provides for His Household

God is wise and smart. He does not spare his blessings in managing his household, knowing that it is a way to attain the goal of the best management of his household – his people. God is always willing to provide anything for his household, like human parents. Abraham was the first person who experienced God the provider (Jehovah-Jireh). In his conversation with Isaac on their way to Mt. Moriah, Abraham answers his son, Isaac when he is asked, "Where is the lamb for the burnt offering": "God will provide the lamb for the burnt offering, my son." (Genesis 22:8). When Abraham showed his love of God more than anything else, the angel of God stopped him killing his son. And like his confession of "God will provide," Abraham found a ram caught by its horns in a thicket and sacrificed it as a burnt offering instead of his son. He called that place "The LORD Will Provide (=Jehovah-Jireh)" (Genesis 22:14).

Jesus in Matthew 6:25-34 tells us not to worry about our life, what we will eat or drink; or about our body, what we will wear. Jesus tells his disciples about God who provides: "[31]Therefore do not be anxious, saying, 'What shall we eat?' or 'What shall we drink?' or 'What shall we wear?' [32]For the Gentiles seek all these things; and your heavenly Father knows that you need them all" (Matthew 6:31-32).

### God Feeds His Household

When the whole community grumble against Moses and Aaron in the desert about food, God tells Moses in Exodus 16:4-5: "Behold, I will rain bread from heaven for you; and the people shall go out and gather a day's portion every day, that I may prove them, whether they will walk in my law or not. On the sixth day, when they prepare what they bring in, it will be twice as much as they gather daily." God fed the Israelites with manna and quail.

God's people may ask God for daily food, believing that God feeds us. Agur in Proverbs 30:7-8 asks God: "[7]Two things I ask of thee; deny them not to me before I die: [8]Remove far from me falsehood and lying; give me neither poverty nor riches, feed me with the food that is needful for me." Jesus also teaches the Lord's prayer to his disciples, in which we ask God, "Give us today our daily bread." (Matthew 6:11; Luke 11:3). By asking God for daily bread in our prayer, we acknowledge that God feeds us every day.

Jesus proclaims that he is the bread of life. Jesus in John 6:32 says: "For the bread of life is he who comes down from heaven and gives life to the world"; in John 6:35: "I am the bread of life. He who comes to me will never go hungry, and he who believes in me will never be thirsty"; in John 6:48-51: "I am the bread of life. … I am the living bread that came down from heaven. If anyone eats of this bread, he will live forever." Jesus, "I AM" (Ἐγώ εἰμι, egó eimi), had come down to earth to give us eternal life.

## God Guides/Leads His Household

God guides or walks with Enoch, Noah, Abraham, Isaac, Jacob, Joseph, and Moses and the Israelites since their exodus from Egypt. God guides the Israelites in front of them. Exodus 13:21-22 states: "And the LORD went before them by day in a pillar of cloud to lead them along the way, and by night in a pillar of fire to give them light, that they might travel by day and by night; the pillar of cloud by day and the pillar of fire by night did not depart from before the people." The psalmist in Psalm 48:14 confesses: "For this God is our God for ever and ever; he will be our guide even to the end." Jesus in Matthew 28:20 promises us to be with us: "And surely I am with you always, to the very end of the age" as Jesus Christ is Immanuel (= God is with us).

## God Protects His Household

God protects people in his household. Although Adam and Eve fell, God protects them by making garments of skin for Adam and his wife and clothed them. God protected Noah, Abraham, Isaac, Jacob, Joseph, and the Israelites in their journeys. The psalmist in Psalm 18:2

states: "The Lord is my rock, my protection, my Savior. My God is my rock. I can run to him for safety"; in Psalm 46:1-3: "[1]God is our protection (refuge) and our strength. He always helps in times of trouble. [2]So, we will not be afraid even if the earth shakes, or the mountains fall into the sea, [3]even if the oceans roar and foam, or the mountains shake at the raging sea"; and in Psalm 144:2: "He protects me like a strong, walled city, and he loves me. He is my defender and my Savior, my shield and my protection." (NCV) David and other psalmists describe God in their psalms as מָגֵן (magen, shield: Psalm 3:3, 7:11, 18:2, 18:30, 18:35, 28:7, 33:20, 89:18, 115:9-11, 119:114, 144:2),[1] מַחֲסֶה (machaseh, refuge, shelter, protection: Psalm 14:6, 46:1, 61:3, 62:7, 62:8, 71:7, 73:28, 91:2, 91:9, 94:22, 104:18, 142:5),[2] מָצוּד (matsuwd, stronghold, fortress: Psalm 18:2, 31:2-3, 66:11, 71:3, 91:2, 144:2),[3] and/or מִשְׂגָּב (misgab, high tower, stronghold, refuge: Psalm 9:9, 18:2, 46:7, 46:11, 48:3, 59:9, 59:16, 59:17, 62:2, 62:6, 94:22, 144:2).[4] God is our shield, refuge, and stronghold/fortress, who protects us and let us escape to him from all dangers. He covers us with his feathers, we are safe under his wings (Psalm 17:8, 91:4).

## God Helps His Household

God helps his people in his household whenever they ask for his help. 1 Samuel 7:12 states: "Then Samuel took a stone and set it up, and called its name 'Ebene'zer,' (אֶבֶן הָעֵזֶר, stone of the help) for he said, 'Hitherto the LORD has helped us." God helped his people – Noah, Abraham, Isaac, Jacob, Joseph, Moses, Joshua, and the Israelites – in their journeys so that they were not stumbled and did not go astray. The Psalmist in Psalm 46:4-5 exhorts: "There is a river whose streams make glad the city of God, the holy habitation of the Most High. God is in the midst of her, she shall not be moved; God will help her right early." God is always there to help his people whenever they reach out

---

[1] Strong's Hebrew Concordance, "4043. magen or meginnah." *BibleHub.* Retrieved from https://biblehub.com/hebrew/4043.htm

[2] Ibid., "4268. machaseh or machseh." *BibleHub.* Retrieved from https://biblehub.com/hebrew/4268.htm

[3] Ibid., "4686. matsuwd." *BibleHub.* Retrieved from https://biblehub.com/hebrew/4686.htm

[4] Ibid., "4869. misgab." *BibleHub.* Retrieved from https://biblehub.com/hebrew/4869.htm

their hands for help as God is Jehovah-Shammah (יְהוָה-שָׁמָּה, The LORD is there) as is in Ezekiel 48:35. God is near us even today and is willing to help us whenever we ask him for help.

Jesus was willing to help people whenever they came to him. He never rejected people who came to him to be healed, comforted, or helped. The coming Christ was depicted as 'Wonderful Counselor' in Isaiah 9:6. Jesus considers himself "the Helper" and thus tells his disciples in John 14:16: "I will pray the Father, and he will give you another Counselor (= Helper), to be with you forever"; in 14:26: "But the Counselor (= Helper), the Holy Spirit, whom the Father will send in my name, he will teach you all things, and bring to your remembrance all that I have said to you." As Jesus promised his disciples, the Holy Spirit came upon us as another Helper and leads us in the right direction.

### God Heals His Household

God heals his people's wounds when they come to him. God tells the Israelites in Exodus 15:26: "If you will diligently hearken to the voice of the LORD your God, and do that which is right in his eyes, and give heed to his commandments and keep all his statutes, I will put none of the diseases upon you which I put upon the Egyptians; for I am the LORD, your healer (יְהוָה-רֹפְאֶךָ, Jehovah-Rophekha)." The psalmist in Psalm 103:2-3 praises God: "Bless the LORD, O my soul and forget not all his benefits, who forgives all your iniquity, who heals all your diseases;" in Psalm 147:3: "He heals the brokenhearted and binds up their wounds." Hosea exhorts the Israelites in Hosea 6:1: "Come, let us return to the LORD; for he has torn, that he may heal us; he has stricken, and he will bind us up." God heals his people not only their physical wounds but also spiritual wounds.

Luke in his Gospel emphasizes Jesus' healing ministry. It seems to be natural that Luke as a physician was interested in Jesus' healing of people who came to him (Luke 6:6-11, 7:1-17, 7:21, 8:26-56, 9:37-43, 13:10-17, 14:1-6, 17:11-19, 18:35-43). Jesus' healing is continuous work of God's healing as Jehovah-Rapha (The LORD heals). Jesus' healing ministry is an important part of the economy of God that takes a good care of his people and was succeeded by his disciples (Acts 3:1-10, 9-32-43, 20:7-12).

## God Teaches/Instructs His Household

God teaches his people that each of them can manage his/her own household successfully. God tells Moses in Exodus 4:12: "Now therefore go, and I will be with your mouth and teach you what you shall speak." Isaiah 54:13 states: "All your sons shall be taught by the LORD, and great shall be the prosperity of your sons." The psalmist in Psalm 71:17 confesses: "O God, from my youth thou hast taught me, and I still proclaim thy wondrous deeds." The Hebrew word, יָרָה (yarah or yara), means teach, instruct, or direct.[5] The noun form, Torah (תּוֹרָה), is from this verb, יָרָה (yarah or yara). It literally means instruction or teaching and generally refers to Moses' five books, Pentateuch (Genesis to Deuteronomy) and is translated as "Law." Torah also refers to the oral tradition of Law and more widely refers to God's instructions in the Old Testament.

Teaching, along with healing, is an important part of Jesus' public ministry. He taught his disciples about the kingdom of God. Even after he was resurrected, Jesus taught his disciples about the kingdom of God during forty days before his ascension (Acts 1:3). Jesus commanded his disciples in Matthew 28:19-20: "Go therefore and make disciples of all nations, baptizing them …, teaching them to oversee all that I have commanded you." We as his disciples continue to teach people to bring them to God's household.

## God Gives a Victory to His Household

God wants his people to win the victory in their life. By winning a battle or a war, each person in God's household can maximize his/her satisfaction. God let his people win the battles – the Israelites defeated while they were marching toward the land of Canaan, in the land of Canaan, etc." When Moses defeated Amalek in Exodus 17:8-16, he built an altar and called the name of it, "The LORD is my banner (=

---

[5] Ibid., "3384. yarah or yara." *BibleHub*. Retrieved from https://biblehub.com/hebrew/3384.htm

Jehovah-Nissi)" (v. 15) as God gave the Israelites a miraculous victory in the fight against Amalek.

Paul in 1 Corinthians 15:56-57 states: "The sting of death is sin, and the power of sin is the law. But thanks be to God, who gives us the victory through our Lord Jesus Christ." Paul encourages us to fight a good fight, believing that God will give us the victory: "I have fought to the good fight, I have finished the race, I have kept the faith. Henceforth there is laid up for me the crown of righteousness, which the Lord, the righteous judge, will award to me on that Day, and not only to me but also to all who have loved his appearing" (2 Tim. 4:7-8).

**God's Governing Activities**

The economy of God in the Bible – the Old Testament and the New Testament – can be defined as God's governing and/or managing activities of his household, including beginning of his household by creating it, blessing people of his household, providing their needs, feeding them, guiding/leading them, protecting them, teaching/instructing them, and giving them a victory in their fight against the evil power, etc. The purpose of the economy of God as we saw at the beginning of this chapter is to let his people "be fruitful, multiply, and fill the earth."

# Chapter Three

# Food

## God's Provision of Food

Why do people make money? They earn money to eat food, wear clothes, and dwell in a place. Nobody can live without food. Food is indispensable for people's economic activity. God provided his people with food at the very beginning of creation. He also provided every living creature with food. The initial food that God provided was green plants but not meat, yet.

God in Genesis 1:29-30 says: "[29]I have given you every plant yielding seed which is upon the face of all the earth, and every tree with seed in its fruit; you shall have them food. [30]And to every beast of the earth, and to every bird of the air, and to everything that creeps on the earth, everything that has the breath of life, I have given every green plant for food." God in Genesis 9:3-4 extended food for his people and included meat for Noah and his family: "[3]Every moving thing that lives shall be food for you; and as I gave you the green plants, I give you everything. [4]Only you shall not eat flesh with its life, that is, its blood." God did not allow his people to eat flesh with blood as blood means life that belongs only to God.

When the Israelites marched in the wilderness after they left Egypt, they ran out of food. The Israelites grumbled and complained against Moses and Aaron. Then, God provided them with manna and quail – food that came down from heaven. God in Exodus 16:12 says to Moses: "I have heard the murmurings of the people of Israel; say to them, 'At twilight you shall eat flesh, and in the morning, you shall be filled with bread; then you shall know that I am the LORD your God.'" God in Leviticus 11 gave Moses and the Israelites a dietary law (a law on food), telling them what they can eat and what they cannot eat. God distinguished clean food from unclean food and let his people eat only clean food which seemed to be healthier food from today's medical perspective.

Scott Munger points out that food shows our dependence on God and makes us humble before God.[6] Deuteronomy 8:3 states: "And he humbled you and let you hunger and fed you with manna, which you did not know, nor did your fathers know; that he might make you know that man does not live by bread alone, but that man lives by everything that proceeds out of the mouth of the LORD." That is, God provides us with food not only for our body but also more importantly for our spirit – the spiritual food, the word of God.

**God's Invitation to Life**

God in Isaiah 55:1-2 invites people to the waters, the source of life: "[1]Ho, everyone who thirsts, come to the waters; and he who has no money, come, buy and eat! Come, buy wine and milk without money and without price. [2]Why do you spend your money for that which is not bread, and your labor for that which does not satisfy?" We can get food and drink when we come to God with our humble mind even without money and without price. God is willing to provide food and drink to them who come to him, the source of life.

**Jesus the Bread of Life**

Jesus also teaches the Lord's prayer to his disciples, in which we ask God, "Give us today our daily bread." (Matthew 6:11; Luke 11:3). Jesus proclaims that he is the bread of life. Jesus in John 6:32 says: "For the bread of life is he who comes down from heaven and gives life to the world"; in John 6:35: "I am the bread of life. He who comes to me will never go hungry, and he who believes in me will never be thirsty"; in John 6:48-51: "I am the bread of life. … I am the living bread that came down from heaven. If anyone eats of this bread, he will live forever."

As we read in Matthew 14:13-21, Mark 6:30-44, Luke 9:10-17, and John 6:1-13, Jesus fed five thousand men (besides women and children) with five loaves of bread and two fish. After they all ate enough, Jesus' disciples gathered the pieces that were left over and filled twelve

---

[6] S. Munger, "The Bible and Food," *All About God.* Retrieved from https://www.allaboutgod.com/the-bible-and-food.htm.

baskets. On another occasion that is recorded in Matthew 15:32-39 and Mark 8:1-10, Jesus fed four thousand men (besides women and children) with seven loaves of bread. After they all ate and were satisfied, the disciples picked up seven basketfuls of broken pieces that were left over. Jesus the bread of life fed people who came to him. Although earthly resources are limited and scarce, God the source of life provides food to his people sufficiently.

Food is essential in our daily living, but Jesus tells us not to worry about food, drink, and clothes. Jesus in Matthew 6:25 says: "Therefore I tell you, do not be anxious about your life, what you shall eat or what you shall drink; nor about your body, what you shall put on. Is not life more than food, and the body more than clothing?"; and repeated in 6:31: "Therefore do not be anxious, saying, 'What shall we eat?' or 'What shall we drink?' or 'What shall we wear?' When we belong to the household of God, God as the head of his household provides us with food. As we saw in Chapter 2, providing or feeding food to his people is a very important God's governing or economic activity.

**Debate on the Dietary Law**

In the early Christian community, there was a debate on the Jewish dietary law which God had provided for the Israelites in the Old Testament (Leviticus 11) as the Gentiles joined the Christian community although the Jews and the Gentiles lived separately. So, a resolution for the Gentile Christians who did not observe the Jewish dietary law was necessary and a letter from the Jerusalem Council was sent to Gentile believers in which Gentile believers were to abstain from food sacrificed to idols, from blood, from the meat of strangled animals, and from sexual immorality, as James, the head of the Jerusalem Council and Jesus' physical brother, suggested (Acts 15:20 & 29).

## Unclean Food and the Gentiles

Peter in Acts 10 saw a vision three times while he was falling into a trance. Peter saw the heaven opened and something like a large sheet came down. It contained all kinds of unclean animals and reptiles and birds of the air. And a voice told him, "Get up, Peter, kill and eat." (Acts 10:13). Peter replied, "Surely not, Lord! I have never eaten anything impure or unclean." (Acts 10:14) The voice told Peter, "Do not call anything impure that God has made clean." This happened three times, and then the sheet was immediately taken back to heaven. All kinds of unclean food that were contained in the sheet in Peter's vision was referred to the Gentiles, particularly Cornelius and his family in Acts 10. And this is the beginning of Peter's and other Jewish Christians' association with the Gentiles for the purpose of gospel.

## Food Offered to Idols

Although the resolution that was made by the Jerusalem Council prohibited the Gentile Christians from eating food that was offered to idols, the Gentile Christians could not distinguish the food that was not offered to idols from the food that was offered to idols in the market. So, some Gentile Christians would eat food which they purchased in the market with a guilty feeling (Romans 14:23; 1 Cor. 8:7). Paul further clarified on the matter of food for those weak Christians. Paul in Romans 14:17 says: "For the kingdom of God is not food and drink but righteousness and peace and joy in the Holy Spirit." The kingdom of God is not about food and drink, so it is okay that you can eat anything that is purchased in the market, without knowing whether or the food was sacrificed to idols. However, if your eating becomes a stumbling block to weak Christians, "it is right not to eat meat or drink wine or do anything that makes your brother stumble." (Romans 14:21). Paul in 1 Corinthians 8:13 goes one step further regarding food: "Therefore, if food is a cause of my brother's falling, I will never eat meat, lest I cause my brother to fall." This is our love for our brothers and sisters whom God loves and accepts.

## Food in Holy Communion

Jesus in his last supper with his disciples took the bread, gave thanks, and broke it, and gave it to his disciples, saying: "This is my body which is given for you. Do this in remembrance of me" (Luke 22:19; 1 Cor. 11:24). In the same way, after the supper he took the cup (of wine), saying: "This cup which is poured out for you is the new covenant in my blood" (Luke 22:20; 1 Cor. 11:25). Every time Christians participate in holy communion, they are aware that Jesus Christ's body was broken and his blood was shed to provide them with eternal food.

# Chapter Four

# Land

Resources include land, labor, and capital. Land is also called natural resource, and labor human resource. Why do we need land? We sow seeds and harvest farm products, or build a factory and produce goods, or build a house to reside. We buy or sell land. Land is considered an item for investment.

## The Garden of Eden

The garden of Eden was the first land that God placed the first human beings, Adam and Eve. Genesis 2:8 says: "And the LORD God planted a garden in Eden, in the east, and there he put the man whom he had formed"; and Genesis 2:15 states: "The LORD GOD took the man and put him in the garden of Eden to till (work) it and keep it." The garden of Eden, the original paradise, was already a beautiful and fertile land that contained various animals, vegetables, plants, and trees that bear much fruit. The garden of Eden was unlimited in its products and there was no scarcity problem of natural resource when God planted and blessed the land and let the first human beings reside there.

God in Genesis 2:16b-17 says to Adam before he made Eve: "[16b]You may freely eat of every tree of the garden; [17]but of the tree of knowledge of good and evil you shall not eat, for in the day that you eat of it you shall die." Although the garden belonged to God, the first human beings were not short in their eating in God's land other than the prohibition of eating of the tree of knowledge of good and evil.

When Adam and Eve disobeyed God and ate the fruit of the tree tempted by the serpent, they lost their place in the garden of Eden. Genesis 3:24 states: "He(=God) drove out the man; and at the east of the garden of Eden he placed the cherubim, and a flaming sword which turned every way, to guard the way to the tree of life." Adam and Eve probably went to east after they were expelled from the garden as God placed the cherubim at the east of the garden to prevent their return.

But God still was connected with the life of Adam and Eve and their children. Cain and Abel brought their products as an offering to the LORD in Genesis 4. After Cain killed his brother Abel, Cain went away from God's presence and in the land of Nod, east of Eden – this probably was further away to east from the garden (Genesis 4:16).

### The Land of Ur of the Chaldeans

After the great flood, Noah's three sons multiplied, and their descendants filled the earth. They formed the nations and spread the earth (Genesis 10). After the incidence of the tower of Babel, God scattered them further over the face of the whole earth (Genesis 11:9). Terah, Shem's descendant and Abraham's father lived in Ur of the Chaldeans when God called Abraham to make him the father of many nations (Genesis 11).

God called Abraham while he was in Ur of the Chaldeans (the land of Iraq today) (Genesis 11:31). However, Abraham and his family's journey to Canaan was slow as his father Terah was old. They came to Haran (the land of Turkey today) on their way to Canaan and settled there (Genesis 11:31). Terah died in Haran at the age of 205 (Genesis 11:32).

### The Land of Canaan

Then, God called Abraham (again) in Genesis 12:1, saying: "Leave your country and your kindred and your father' house to the land that I will show you." Abraham departed from Haran when he was 75 years old (Genesis 12:4). Abraham arrived at Canaan, but the land was not given to him (Genesis 12:5-7). Genesis 12:7 states: "Then the LORD appeared to Abram, and said, 'To your descendants I will give this land.'" God repeated his promise of the land to Abraham whenever he appeared to him (Genesis 12:7, 13:15, 15:7, 15:18, 17:8, 24:7).

The only portion of land in Canaan that Abraham could possess was the land that he purchased from Ephron a Hittite for his wife Sarah's burial in Genesis 23. Genesis 23:19-20 states: "[19]After this, Abraham buried Sarah his wife in the cave of the field of Mach-pelah east of Mamre (that is, Hebron) in the land of Canaan. [20]The field and the cave that is in it were made over to Abraham as a possession for a burying place by the Hittites." This allowance seems to be God's deposit or down payment for his promise of the land to Abraham. God put his Spirit in our hearts as a deposit (NIV) or a down payment (CEB) or the first installment (NLT), guaranteeing everything that God has promised us, including the inheritance of the kingdom of God (2 Cor. 1:22; Ephesians 1:14). A deposit or a down payment is frequently used by a buyer to show his/her will of purchasing a house or land for sure. Abraham's son, Isaac, and his son Jacob and their families resided in Canaan as sojourners until they moved to Egypt, where Joseph, Jacob's son already became a prime minister.

## The Land of Egypt

Land was very important as it would connect God with his people. Jacob was worried about moving to Egypt when the land of Canaan suffered from famine and he became to know that Joseph was prime minister in Egypt. Then, God appeared to Jacob in a vision and told him: "Jacob, Jacob. I am God, the God of your father; do not be afraid to go down to Egypt; for I will there make you a great nation. I will go down with you to Egypt, and I will also bring you up again; and Joseph's hand will close your eyes." (Genesis 46:2-4, RSV) God already had told Abraham that his descendants would stay there as strangers, would be enslaved, and mistreated four hundred years before they would obtain the land of Canaan (Genesis 15:13-14). Yet, God promised Jacob that he would be with Jacob and his family.

The number of Jacob's family, including Joseph, who moved to Egypt was 70 (Genesis 46:27; 75 people in Acts 7:14). While Joseph was alive, the Egyptians did not look down upon Jacob and his family. However, after Joseph died and his name was forgotten, the Israelites/Hebrews became slaves, doing hard labor in brick and mortar and other mundane work. The Israelites had spent in Egypt for 430 years without hope. People forgot their ancestors' God. But God never forgot his people and his promise with Abraham to give the land of Canaan to his descendants in Genesis 12:7.

## The Land of Canaan, Again

God told Moses in Exodus 3:17: "I promise that I will bring you up out of the affliction of Egypt, to the land of the Canaanites, the Hittites, the Amorites, the Perizzites, the Hivites, and the Jebusites, a land of flowing milk and honey." The Israelites wandered around for forty years in the wilderness because of their unbelief before they entered the land of Canaan. Moses could not enter the land of Canaan, but Joshua led the Israelites after Moses. Joshua and the Israelites could cross the river Jordan and continued to conquer cities.

## Division of the Land

The distribution of the land was already ordered through Moses by God even before the Israelites entered the land. God in Numbers 26:53-56 told Moses: "53To these the land shall be divided for inheritance according to the number of names. 54To a large tribe you shall give a large inheritance, and to a small tribe you shall give a small inheritance; every tribe shall be given its inheritance according to its numbers. 55But the land shall be divided by lot; according to the names of the tribes of their fathers they shall inherit. 56Their inheritance shall be divided according to a lot between the larger and the smaller."

God's instruction for the division of the land was according to the size of the tribes and by lot. The Israelites would accept lot as God's will. God tried to be fair among all tribes and reduce their complaints. After Joshua and the Israelites mostly conquered the land of Canaan, he divided the land according to God's instruction (Joshua 13:8-19:51). After Joshua and the Israelites had finished dividing the land into its allotted portions, the Israelites gave Joshua an inheritance among them as God had commanded (Joshua 20:49). Then, the Levites (the descendants of Kohath, Gershon, and Merari) who were omitted from the division of the land were given 48 towns for their basic pasturelands (42) and refuge (6) as God had commanded through Moses (Numbers 35:1-8; Joshua 21).

## Cultivation of the Land

God in Leviticus 25:2 says to the Israelites through Moses: "When you come into the land which I give you, the land shall keep a sabbath to the LORD." The Israelites would plant their fields, prune their vineyard, and harvest their crops for six years. But in the seventh year, the land was supposed to have a sabbath of rest. The Israelites were not supposed to sow their field and prune their vineyard.

God told the Israelites not to reap what grows of itself or harvest the grapes of their untended vine as the land is to have a rest (Leviticus 25:5). However, whatever the land yielded during the sabbath year would be for God's people, their household, and for their livestock and wild animals in their land (Leviticus 25:6).

## Ownership of the Land

The primary ownership of all land belonged to God in the Old Testament. It seems to be obvious as God had created the heavens and earth. Moses in Exodus 9:29 says to Pharaoh: "... that you may know that the earth is the LORD's." Moses in Deuteronomy 10:14 says to the Israelites: "Behold, to the LORD your God belong heaven and the heaven of heavens, the earth with all that is in it."

The secondary ownership of land was given to God's people, but they were not allowed to sell their land "permanently" as all land belonged to God. Although they sold land out of poverty, they were supposed to purchase their land back. If they could not repurchase their land, the nearest relative purchased the land on behalf of them. If they could not repurchase the land, the land would remain in the possession of the buyer until the Year of Jubilee. In the Year of Jubilee, the land will be returned, and the person could go back to his property (Leviticus 25:23-28). God in Leviticus 25:23-24 says: "The land shall not be sold in perpetuity, for the land is mine; for you are strangers and sojourners with me. And in all the country you possess, you shall grant a redemption of the land."

## Redemption of the Land

God in Leviticus 25:25 says: "If one of your fellow Israelites becomes poor and sells some of their property, their nearest relative is to come and redeem what they have sold." The nearest relative of the poor who would redeem (=buy) the land was called a "redeemer" (גֹּאֵל, goel in Hebrew).

Elimelech and Naomi with his two sons and their wives in the Book of Ruth lost their land in Bethlehem when there was a famine and went to Moab. Elimelech and his two sons died in Moab. Later, Naomi and her daughter-in-law returned to Bethlehem. When the nearest kinsman refused to redeem the land (on the condition of marrying Ruth), Boaz, the second nearest kinsman, accepted to redeem the land of Elimelech (Ruth 4). So, Boaz became the redeemer for Naomi and Ruth and took Ruth as his wife. Boaz as the redeemer is a type for Jesus Christ who had come to us as the nearest kinsman, wearing human flesh, to redeem the land that Adam and Eve had lost when they fell.

Jesus calls Satan "the ruler of this world" (John 12:31, 16:11) as he obtained the power of this earth for the time being since Adam and Eve fell. Paul calls Satan "the prince of the power of the air" (Ephesians 2:2). Paul in 1 Corinthians 6:19-20 says: "[19]Do you not know that your body is a temple of the Holy Spirit within you, which you have from God? You are not your own; [20]you were bought (=redeemed) with a price. So, glorify God in your body."; and in Titus 2:14: "who gave himself for us to redeem us from all iniquity and to purify for himself a people of his own who are zealous for good deeds." Jesus Christ redeemed (=purchased) us – our life and land that we had lost when Adam and Eve fell at the cost of his blood that was shed on the cross. Jesus became the Redeemer for us.

## Chapter Five

# Labor

Labor is another important resource, which is also called human resource. God's six-day creation is labor or work (**מְלַאכְתּוֹ**, mela-kuto, his work, Genesis 2:2, 3),[7] and God rested on the seventh day (Genesis 2:2-3). The same Hebrew word, **מְלַאכְתּוֹ** (mela-kuto), is also used in connection with people's work (Genesis 39:11; 1 Kings 7:14; 2 Chronicles 16:5; Nehemiah 4:15). The beginning of the economy of God is God's blessings on human beings who were created according to the image and likeness of God.

**Beginning of Labor**

The Hebrew word for 'till' or 'work' is **עָבַד** (abad), which means 'serve,' 'labor,' 'work,' or 'cultivate.'[8] The word **עָבַד** (abad) is used in Genesis 2:5 before God made (or formed) Adam (Genesis 2:7): "… and there was no man to till (or cultivate) the ground." The first record of a human's labor/work is in Genesis 2:15: "The LORD God took the man and put him in the garden of Eden to till (work, NIV) it and keep it." Adam's labor (or service) of cultivating and taking care of the ground, plants, and trees in the garden of Eden also means serve God as his steward or servant. Serving or laboring or cultivating the ground, plants, and trees in the garden of Eden was surely God's blessing on Adam. He probably enjoyed his labor. His labor was not hard and burdensome.

Then, Adam and Eve fell as they ate (the fruit) of the tree of knowledge of good and evil. God says to the woman (Eve) in Genesis 3:16: "I will greatly multiply your pain in childbearing; in pain you shall bring forth children, yet your desire shall be for your husband, and he shall rule

---

[7] Strong's Hebrew Concordance, "4399. melakah," *BibleHub*. Retrieved from https://biblehub.com/hebrew/4399.htm

[8] Ibid., "5647. abad," *BibleHub*. Retrieved from https://biblehub.com/hebrew/5647.htm

over you." A process of childbirth is called "labor" as it is very painful. If Adam and Eve had not fallen and thus there had not been God's curse, a woman's childbirth would have been much easier without pain.

God says to the man (Adam) in Genesis 3:17-19: "[17]Because you listened to the voice of your wife, have eaten of the tree of which I commanded, 'You shall not eat of it,' cursed is the ground because of you; in toil you shall eat of it all the days of your life; [18]thorns and thistles it shall bring forth to you; and you shall eat the plants of the field. [19]In the sweat of your face you shall eat bread till you return to the ground, for out of it you were taken; you are dust, and to dust you shall return."

**Is Labor God's Blessing or Curse?**

M. Douglas Meeks mentions that there are two opposed views of work or labor – a curse and a blessing.[9] Is labor God's blessing or curse? The Hebrew word, **עִצָּבוֹן** (itstsabon), is a 'pain,' 'toil,' or 'painful toil.'[10] The Hebrew word, **עִצָּבוֹן** (itstsabon), also means 'grief,' that is, 'hard and continuous work' or 'exhausting labor.' When you compare the two different words, **עָבַד**(abad) and **עִצָּבוֹן** (itstsabon), the first one is your willing labor as God's steward whereas the second one is your painful labor to survive. The first one is God's blessing as he placed the man to take care of his creation – ground, trees, and plants whereas the second one is God's curse as he should labor painfully in the sweat of his face to eat bread.

**God's Instruction on Labor**

God in Exodus 20:9-11 says: "[9]Six days you shall labor, and do all your work; [10]but the seventh day is a sabbath to the LORD your God; in it you shall not do any work, you, or your son, or your daughter, your manservant, or your maidservant, or your cattle, or the sojourner who is within your gates; [11]for in six days the LORD made heaven and earth, the sea, and all that is in them, and rested the seventh day; therefore the LORD blessed the sabbath day and hallowed it." So, God's

---

[9] M. D. Meeks, *God The Economist*. Fortress Press, 1989 (1946), 128-130.

[10] Strong's Hebrew Concordance, "6093. itstsabon," *BibleHub*. Retrieved from https://biblehub.com/hebrew/6093.htm

creatures – human beings and cattle – shall labor for six days but rest on the seventh day because God labored for his creation for six days and rested on the seventh day. The Hebrew word for "labor" here is עָבַד (abad) – the positive connotation of labor. The Hebrew word עָבַד (abad) may be equivalent to the Greek word οἰκονομέω (oikonomeo, the verb form of οἰκονομία, oikonomía), that is 'labor/manage as a steward/servant of God's household.'

Ecclesiastes 5:18-19 states: "[18]Behold, what I have seen to be good and to be fitting is to eat and drink and find enjoyment in all the toil with which one toils under the sun the few days of his life which God has given him, for this is his lot. [19]Every man also to whom God has given wealth and possessions and power to enjoy them, and to accept his lot and find enjoyment in his toil-this is the gift of God." A man's toil/labor may be hard, but God allows him wealth, possessions, and ability to enjoy them. So, when a man is happy in his labor that may result in wealth and possessions, his labor that God allows him is God's gift along with his wealth and possessions.

## Jesus' Labor on the Sabbath

What is the boundary of labor for Jewish people? Any small movement of one's body is considered labor. When you stay at a hotel in Israel on Friday evening or Saturday, you may notice that an elevator door is automatically opened and closed on every floor. The orthodox Jews observe the Sabbath starting Friday evening until Saturday evening. On the Sabbath they do not labor. They do not even push a button of an elevator thinking that this is a kind of labor. If an elevator is not being operated automatically and yet a Jew wants to push a button of the floor that he should get off, he will ask a person who is not a Jew in the elevator. Even today they try to keep the rules and regulations for the Sabbath that their ancestors had made long time ago. Should believers not work at all on a sabbath day even for good-will work? This caused a debate between Jesus and the Jewish leaders, the Pharisees and the scribes (and the Sadducees), in the Gospels.

In Matthew 12:1-8 (also Mark 2:23-28 and Luke 6:1-5) Jesus and his disciples went through the grain fields on the Sabbath. His disciples were hungry and began to pluck heads of grain and ate. The Pharisees saw this and criticized Jesus and his disciples due to their 'labor' (plucked heads of grain). On the Sabbath, God's people are supposed to do honor/worship God while they take a rest. The Jewish leaders made many rules and regulations of how they should observe the Sabbath, which God did not instruct them to do. The Jewish leaders defined what kind of labor is prohibited on the Sabbath. So, according to their rules and regulations, even minor labor was not supposed to do (like Jesus' disciples plucking heads of grains). According to the Pharisees' interpretation of the Law, nobody can labor on the Sabbath. Everybody should take a rest. Jesus' interpretation of 'keep the Sabbath holy' does not reject his disciples' small labor (of plucking) to solve the hunger problem. Then, Jesus claimed that "For the Son of man is lord of the Sabbath" (Matthew 12:8). God gave his people the Sabbath to take a rest from their labor and honor/worship God. The Sabbath is for his people not his people for the Sabbath. Worshipping God includes not only ritual worship but also spiritual worship, that is, glorifying God by saving other person's life or helping other people who are desperately in need. Jesus always emphasized the intent of the Law, the meaning behind the letter. The Pharisees were so concerned about religious rituals that they missed the whole purpose of the Temple.

In Matthew 12:9-14 (also Mark 3:1-6 and Luke 6:6-11) Jesus met a man with a withered hand. The Pharisees asked Jesus in Matthew 12:10: "Is it lawful to heal on the sabbath?" Jesus answered them in Matthew 12:11-12: "[11]What man of you, if he has one sheep and it falls into a pit on the sabbath, will not lay hold of it and lift it out? [12]Of how much more value is a man than a sheep! So, it is lawful to do good (work) on the Sabbath." Then, Jesus healed the man with a withered hand. Jesus sometimes intentionally healed the people who came to him on the Sabbath.

His intention was to make people know the true meaning of the Sabbath. God told his people through Moses in Exodus 20:8 (and in Deuteronomy 5:12): "Remember the Sabbath day by keeping it holy." On the Sabbath day or now on Sunday, God's people worship God with their whole heart, whole soul, and whole strength. Believers take a rest without labor, giving thanks to God by remembering his creation, protection, and salvation of us. Yet, if there is someone who needs your help, you may labor to help the person. Jesus tells us in Mark 2:27:

"The Sabbath was made for man, not man for the Sabbath." What is the spirit of the Sabbath? On Sunday, which is the Christians' Sabbath, we worship and glorify God remembering his creation of us and salvation of us. At the same time, we may do good by following the example of Jesus.

Although Jewish people kept the Sabbath, it did not give them joy, happiness, comfort, and restoration of soul but more burden, discomfort, and tiredness. Jesus emphasized that he is the Lord of the Sabbath and that doing good (labor) is lawful on the Sabbath. That is, Jesus wants to teach his disciples the true meaning and spirit of the Sabbath. God set us free from all the bondages. We have freedom to choose whatever we want to do even on Sundays within the Christian boundary. Although we do whatever we want, our conduct should be according to God's will to please him.

### Labor as God's Blessing

Although God announced a curse to the woman (Genesis 3:16) and the man (Genesis 3:17-19), labor itself is not a curse from God. Rather, any kind of work for God's household is God's blessings. Especially when you can enjoy your work with all your heart and mind, it is a true blessing from God.

Paul was a tentmaker while he spread the gospel although he was a student or scholar under the prominent Jewish law teacher, Gamaliel (Acts 5:34-39). He was from a rich family.[11] But, Paul took the labor of tent-making to travel around Asia Minor, Macedonia, and other Greek towns/cities. Paul met Priscilla and Aquila (Acts 18), who were also tent-makers. Paul, and Priscilla and Aquila rejoiced in their labor, spread the gospel, together.

Paul in Colossians 3:23 states: "Whatever you do, work at it with all your heart, as working for the Lord, not for human masters." What Paul means here is that although your daily work is for your earthly

---

[11] K. P. Choi, *Paul's Life, Epistles, and the Central Themes of His Theology* (in Korean). Seoul, Korea: Qumran Publishing House, 2013, 21-23.

master, consider that you work for the Lord your God as the one who allowed you to work in this world is God himself.

Paul in 2 Thessalonians 3:10 states: "For even when we were with you, we gave this command: If anyone will not work, let him not eat." The Bible teaches us that labor/work itself is neutral, but when you labor with all your heart as if you work for the Lord, pleasing him with your labor, your labor even for your earthly employer (let alone your labor for the Lord) is holy and blessed by God.

## Chapter Six

# Tithes and Taxes

### Beginning of Tithes

The first tithe in the Bible was the one that Abraham offered to Melchizedek, king of Salem and priest of God Most High when he returned from the defeat of Chedorlaomer and the kings who were with him. Genesis 14:18-20 states: "[18]Then Melchizedek king of Salem brought out bread and wine. He was priest of God Most High, [19]and he blessed Abram, saying, 'Blessed be Abram by God Most High, Creator of heaven and earth. [20]And praise be to God Most High, who delivered your enemies into your hand.' Then Abram gave him a tenth of everything" (also, in Hebrews 7:2-10). The literal translation of 'Melchizedek' is king of righteousness. He was not the high priest in the order of Aaron as he preceded Aaron and did not belong to any tribe of Israel as he was not of Abraham's family. Melchizedek, the eternal high priest as well as king of righteousness and king of peace was a type of Jesus in the Old Testament as the Book of Hebrews describes (Hebrews 5:6-11, 6:20-7:17).

Then, Jacob mentioned a tithe in his prayer to God at Bethel while he was running away from Esau. Genesis 28:20-22 states: "[20]Then Jacob made a vow, saying, 'If God will be with me, and will keep me in this way that I go, and will give me bread to eat and clothing to wear, [21]so that I come again to my father's house in peace, then the LORD shall be my God, [22]and this stone, which I have set up for a pillar, shall be God's house; and of all that thou givest me I will give the tenth to thee." Jacob promised God to offer him a tithe conditionally when God would bless him.

### Purposes of Tithes

A primary reason why God tells his people to offer a tithe to him is to let them know that all things are of God. Although all things belong to God, God takes only the tenth and lets his people live with nine out of ten. Leviticus 27:30 states: "All the tithe of the land, whether of the seed of the land or of the fruit of the trees, is the LORD's; it is holy to the LORD" (also in Leviticus 27:32).

After the Israelites entered the land of Canaan, the land that the Israelites conquered was divided to Jacob's twelve tribes (the Levites were omitted, and Joseph took two portions – Manasseh and Ephraim). The Levites were not allowed to have land, except for 42 towns for them to reside and 6 additional towns of refugee (Numbers 35:1-8; Joshua 21). God wanted the Levites to contribute themselves wholly to their work in the temple. Instead, God arranged them to live with the tithes that were offered by other twelve tribes. That is, the offerings (burnt offerings, grain offerings, fellowship offerings, sin offerings, and guilt offerings) that the Israelites offered were accepted by God, but God let the tithes used for the living of the Levites. God in Numbers 18:21 says: "To the Levites I have given every tithe in Israel for an inheritance, in return for their service in the tent of meeting."; and in Numbers 18:28 (to the Levites): "So shall you also present an offering to the LORD from all your tithes, which you receive from the people of Israel; and from it you shall give the LORD's offering to Aaron the priest."

Practically, the Israelites separated the tithes for the Levites, the Levites separated the tithe of the tithes that they received for the descendants of Aaron. The descendants of Aaron were the end users of the tithes and they did not separate the tenth of what they received. And every third year, the Israelites separated another tenth for the poor Levites, sojourners, orphans, and widows.

Moses in Deuteronomy 14:22-23 states: "[22]You shall tithe all the yield of your seed, which comes forth from the field year by year. [23]And before the LORD your God, in the place which he will choose, to make his name dwell there, you shall eat the tithe of your grain, of your wine, and of your oil, and the firstlings of your herd and flock; that you may learn to fear the LORD your God always."

> The New International Version (NIV): "so that you may learn to revere the LORD your God always." (Deuteronomy 14:23b)

The Good News Translation (GNT): "Do this so that you may learn to honor the LORD your God always." (Deuteronomy 14:23b)

The Living Bible (TLB): "The purpose of tithing is to teach you always to put God first in your lives." (Deuteronomy 14:23b)

As TLB translates it properly, the purpose of tithes is to put God first in our lives and remember that all things belong to God. We should be thankful to God who allows us to use nine out of ten that belong to him.

Moses in Deuteronomy 14:28-29 states: "[28]At the end of every three years you shall bring forth all the tithe of your produce in the same year, and lay it up in your towns; [29]and the Levite, because he has no portion or inheritance with you, and the sojourner, the fatherless, and the widow, who are within your towns, shall come and eat and be filled; that the LORD your God may bless you in all the work of your hands that you do" (also in Deuteronomy 26:12-14). This tithe at the end of every three years was a special one to relieve the Levites, sojourners, orphans, and widows. This is another purpose of tithes to remember the poor neighbors.

When there was a king in Israel, the Israelites had to offer another tenth as taxes to the king, in addition to their tithes for the Levites. God in 1 Samuel 8:15-17 says through Samuel to the Israelites: "[15]He (=King) will take the tenth of your grain and of your vineyards and give it to his officers and to his servants. ... [17]He will take the tenth of your flocks, and you shall be his slaves." 2 Chronicles 31:5-6 states: "[5]As soon as the command (of King Hezekiah) was spread abroad, the people of Israel gave in abundance the first fruits of grain, wine, oil, honey, and of all the produce of the field; and they brought in abundantly the tithe of everything. [6]And the people of Israel and Judah who lived in the cities of Judah also brought in the tithe of cattle and sheep, and the dedicated things which had been consecrated to the Lord their God and laid them in heaps." (also in 2 Chronicles 31:12) Thus, the Israelites separated 13.3% per year of their income before they had a king and 23.3% per year of their income after they had a king: 10% for the Levites, another 10% for the king; and at the end of every three years, 10% (3.3% per year) for the poor Levites, sojourners, orphans, and widows in their towns.

Tithes continued even after the Babylon captivity. Nehemiah 10:37-38 states: "[37]and to bring the first of our coarse meal, and our contributions, the fruit of every tree, the wine and the oil, to the priests, to the chambers of the house of our God; and to bring to the Levites the tithes from our ground, for it is the Levites who collect the tithes in all our rural towns. [38]And the priest, the son of Aaron, shall be with the Levites when the Levites receive the tithes; and the Levites shall bring up the tithe of the tithes to the house of our God, to the chambers, to the storehouse."

## Full Tithes

Malachi 3:8-10 states: "[8]Will man rob God? Yet you are robbing me. But you say, 'How are we robbing thee?' In your tithes and offerings. [9]You are cursed with a curse, for you are robbing me; the whole nation of you. [10]Bring the full tithes into the storehouse, that there may be food in my house; and thereby put me to the test, says the Lord of hosts, if I will not open the windows of heaven for you and pour down for you an overflowing blessing." Offering tithes is not to show off to other people but is a relationship between God and us. What kind or quality of tithes we offer tells us (not others) how much priority we place God in our life.

## Tithes in the New Testament

Jesus in Matthew 23:23 states: "Woe to you, scribes and Pharisees, hypocrites! for you tithe mint and dill and cumin, and have neglected the weightier matters of the law, justice and mercy and faith; these you ought to have done, without neglecting the others." (also, Luke 11:42) Jesus' saying here is equivalent to God's saying in Hosea 6:6: "I desire steadfast love and not sacrifice, the knowledge of God, rather than burnt offerings." God does not mean that he does not want to receive sacrifice and burnt offerings but emphasizes the priority – the practice of steadfast love and knowledge of God are more important than sacrifice and burnt offerings. What Jesus emphasizes in Matthew 23:23

is not a tithe itself but the spirit of tithe – why do you separate a tithe for God? It is to acknowledge that all things belong to God and give thanks to him (by separating the tenth) who allows his people to live with those of God's. Some biblical scholars regard the tithes that God told his people to separate and offer for the Levites as taxes to God under his sovereignty.

## Jesus and Taxes

What was Jesus' attitude toward taxes? When Jesus and his disciples came to Capernaum, the collectors of the half-shekel (or two-drachma) temple tax asked Peter whether Jesus would pay the tax (Matthew 17:24; cf. Exodus 30:13-16). Jesus in Matthew 17:27 says to Peter: "However, not to give offense to them, go to the sea and cast a hook, and take the fish that comes up, and when you open its mouth you will find a shekel; take that and give it to them for me and for yourself." Jesus did not reject the secular rules and regulations although he did not enthusiastically support them.

There is another passage regarding taxes, where the Pharisees tried to entangle Jesus (Matthew 22:15-22; Mark 12:13-17; and Luke 20:20-26). The Pharisees asked Jesus in Matthew 22:17: "Is it lawful to pay taxes to Caesar, or not." Jesus in Matthew 22:21 wisely responded to their malicious question: "Render therefore to Caesar the things that are Caesar's, and to God the things that are God's."

## Christians and Taxes

Paul in Romans 13:6-7 says: "[6]For the same reason you also pay taxes, for the authorities are ministers of God, attending to this very thing. [7]Pay all of them their dues, taxes to whom taxes are due, revenue to whom revenue is due, respect to whom respect is due, honor to whom honor is due." Although the Roman emperor was Nero in his time, Paul tells his fellow Christians to respect the earthly authorities. So, believers should pay taxes duly. Tax avoidance to minimize tax liability within the law by reviewing all the items of tax exemptions and reductions is proper, but tax evasion is illegal and thus Christians are not supposed to do.

### Tithes and Taxes

God used the tithes (taxes that he collected from his people) to provide the Levites with their living as they could wholly devote their time and effort to God at the temple. The Israelites in the Old Testament separated the tenth for God, which was used for the Levites regularly and another tenth for sojourners, orphans, and widows at the end of every three years; and yet another tenth to their king for whom they asked God.

What about today? Some Christians separate and offer the tenth to God at their church, which is used for their pastors' living as well as for the ministry of God, including the relief of the poor people, the support of the local community, missionaries, etc. Their pastors (who are usually not supposed to have a secular job if the church can afford to provide for their living) are equivalent to the Levites in the Old Testament.

All people including Christians pay taxes to the governments – federal, state, and local governments – when they have income and when they purchase goods or services. When people do not have income, they may be supported by the government in the forms of negative income taxes, cash transfers, or in-kind transfers (subsidies by the government), which are similar to the tenth that was separate at the end of every three years in the Old Testament.

When people have income, they pay taxes – the federal income tax and the state income tax, according to their tax brackets. Most people usually pay more than 10% taxes. The federal government's primary source of income is taxes. The taxes that the federal government collects are used for social security, national defense, major health programs, safety net programs (unemployment insurance, food stamps, low-income housing assistance, etc.), interest on the national debt, and others.

As taxes today are used for more various purposes and goals, majority people pay more than 10% taxes, sometimes 30-40% of their income, including the federal income tax, state income tax, social security tax, Medicare tax, and sales tax. God's tax system was a proportional tax system (10% for the Levites and another 10% for the king) whereas the current U.S. tax system is progressive (rich people belong to higher marginal income tax brackets).

## Chapter Seven

# Loans, Interest, And Debts

### God's Instructions on Loans, Interest, and Debts

Individuals or firms may need money for their household or business. The money that they borrow (or lend) is called a loan and the extra money that is charged for the cost of borrowing is called interest. And the money that they should pay back is called a debt. Even in Moses' time, God made provisions for loans. God in Exodus 22:25 instructs the Israelites through Moses: "If you lend money to any of my people with you who is poor, you shall not be to him as a creditor, and you shall not exact interest from him"; and in Deuteronomy 23:19-20: "[19]You shall not lend upon interest to your brother, interest on money, interest on victuals, interest on anything that is lent for interest. [20]To a foreigner you may lend upon interest, but to your brother you shall not lend upon interest; that the LORD your God may bless you in all that you undertake in the land which you are entering to take possession of it."

When a fellow Israelite is poor and wants to borrow money, the Israelites were supposed to lend money without charging any interest. God prohibited the Israelites from charging interest to their fellow Israelites – brothers, relatives, and friends, although they may charge interest to foreigners. Leviticus 25:35-38 states: "[35]And if your brother becomes poor, and cannot maintain himself with you, you shall maintain him; as a stranger and a sojourner he shall live with you. [36]Take no interest from him or increase but fear your God; that your brother may live beside you. [37]You shall not lend him your money at interest, nor give him your food for profit. [38]I am the Lord your God, who brought you forth out of Egypt to give you the land of Canaan and, to be your God." God's instruction for the Israelites regarding loans and interest is consistent throughout the Torah. M. Douglas Meeks explains that high interest charged in the ancient countries often forced debtors to sell themselves into slavery.[12] God probably did not want to see anyone of his people to become a slave again in the land of Canaan, the land of flowing milk and honey, where he was leading them.

Psalm 37:21states: "The wicked borrows, and cannot pay back, but the righteous is generous and gives." Some borrowers may want to take advantage of the lender's good will by not repaying their debts. Even so, God encourages his people's generous lending even if they know some people will not pay back their money. Psalm 112:5 states: "It is well with the man who deals generously and lends, who conducts his affairs with justice." God loves those who give or lend generously and blesses them (2 Corinthians 9:7).

It is interesting to know that God gives examples of a righteous person and an unrighteous person in connection with a lending behavior among several in Ezekiel. An example of a righteous person in Ezekiel 18:8 is: "He does not lend to them (=the hungry and the naked) at interest or take a profit from them"; and in Ezekiel 18:17 is: "He withholds his hand from mistreating the poor and takes no interest or profit from them" (NIV). An example of an unrighteous person in Ezekiel 18:13 is: "He lends at interest (to the poor and the needy) and takes a profit"; and in Ezekiel 22:12 "You take interest and make a profit from the poor. You extort unjust gain from your neighbors" (NIV). A righteous person is willing to help his/her poor and needy neighbors, lending money without interest whereas an unrighteous person wants to take advantage of his/her poor and needy neighbors, lending money at interest and making a profit, which seems to be quite normal today.

## Debts Are Forgiven

A lender expects the money that he lent to be paid back. The borrower should make every effort to pay back the money that he borrowed. What if the borrower cannot pay it back? The lender may want to know why the borrower does not or cannot pay back the money. However,

---

[12] M. D. Meeks, *God The Economist.* Fortress Press, 1989 (1946), 85-86. According to Meeks, "the legal codes of the Near East allowed enormously high interest rates" (p. 85).

God does not want the lender to treat the borrower – the fellow Israelite – too harsh. And at the end of every seven years, the debts shall be forgiven. Deuteronomy 15:1-3 states: "[1]At the end of every seven years you must cancel debts. [2]This is how it is to be done: Every creditor shall cancel any loan they have made to a fellow Israelite. They shall not require payment from anyone among their own people, because the LORD's time for cancelling debts has been proclaimed. [3]You may require payment from a foreigner, but you must cancel any debt your fellow Israelite owes you" (NIV). How can any lender forgive his/her borrower's debt fully at the end of the seventh year? It is because all money/wealth belongs to God not to any individual. So, when God commands us to forgive other people's debts, we are to do so as we are only the delegated or entrusted owners of God's wealth or money. God always pardons our debts and wants us to live the life of forgiveness of others' debts (Matthew 6:14-15).

## Jesus on Loans and Interest

Jesus in Matthew 5:42 says: "Give to him who begs from you, and do not refuse him who would borrow from you." Jesus advises you to lend money to someone when he/she wants to borrow money from you. Of course, when you do not have money, you cannot lend money, however, when you have money, Jesus tells you not to refuse. Yet, this is very difficult as you may also think about a situation that the borrower cannot pay it back. Jesus commands us to do what we cannot do with our natural human mind but can do with the love of Jesus, who loved us unto death even when we were still sinners (Romans 5:8).

Jesus in Luke 6:34-36 goes one step further: "[34]And if you lend to those from whom you hope to receive, what credit is that to you? Even sinners lend to sinners, to receive as much again. [35]But love your enemies, and do good, and lend, expecting nothing in return; and your reward will be great, and you will be sons of the Most High; for he is kind to the ungrateful and the selfish. [36]Be merciful, even as your Father is merciful." How many of us are willing to lend money to our friends without expecting to be repaid? Only a few at most. Then, how many of us are willing to lend money to our enemies – those people whom we do not like or even hate – without expecting to be repaid? Probably close to none. Jesus tells us to do good to our enemies, including lending money to them without expecting to be repaid. Jesus teaches us the absolute goodness – do good all the time to people although they may hurt us or exploit us.

Jesus instructs us that we may lend money or give whatever kind of grace that we have to our enemy – not just fellow Christians – even when we do not expect to get anything back from him/her. Our reward may not be earned on earth but will be accumulated in heaven. And this is a way that we show God's mercy to our enemy through us. By doing so, we may win their souls, bringing them to God. Jesus' teaching here may be connected to Paul's saying in Romans 12:20: "If your enemy is hungry, feed him; if he is thirsty, give him drink; for by so doing you will heap burning coals upon his head." Our good conduct may make them feel shame on what they did to us. However, how many of us can do this absolute goodness to those who try to hard us?

### Debts and Sins

When you borrow money from someone and cannot pay it back on time, you may feel guilty as if you commit sin. That's why the Bible refers sin to debt. Sometimes, debts make you (debtor/borrower) a slave of the creditor/lender. Proverbs 22:7 states: "The rich rules over the poor, and the borrower is the slave of the lender." The borrower may be forced to do anything by the lender until he pays back his debt.

When Peter asked Jesus about forgiveness of sins – how many he should forgive his brother when his brother sins against him, Jesus took the parable of unmerciful servant in Matthew 18:21-35. The servant owed his master 10,000 talents (one talent is equivalent to 5,000-6,000 denarii and one denarius is equivalent to an average worker's one day pay), which is literally unrepayable amount of money although the Bible does not tell how this servant owed this enormous debt to his master. Knowing that his servant could not repay this enormous amount of debt, the master took pity on him, canceled the debt, and let him go free. The servant who was once summoned to his master but then was released met his fellow servant who owed him 100 denarii, which was not a small amount itself; but comparing with 10,000 talents of his debt that was just canceled by his master, it was almost nothing. The servant demanded his fellow servant/debtor to pay it back right away. Then, he put the debtor into prison until he could pay the debt. Having heard this story, the master called the servant in. The master was very much angry about this servant's lack of mercy and turned him over to the jailers to be tortured until he should pay back all he owed, which was impossible. The servant who owed his master 10,000 talents may be each one of us, who could not repay the debt of our sins and trespasses.

Our Master canceled all the debts that we owed when we accepted Jesus as our Savior and when Jesus begged forgiveness of our debts to God on behalf of each one of us. But at the same time, God wants us to forgive our debtors in our daily life. Jesus in Lord's prayer in Matthew 6:12 (compare with Luke 11:4) teaches his disciples how to pray to God: "Forgive us our debts, as we also have forgiven our debtors." Jesus tells us that we should forgive our debtors first to be forgiven our debts by God.

Jesus in Matthew 6:14-15 says: "[14]For if you forgive men their trespasses, your heavenly Father also will forgive you; [15]but if you do not forgive men their trespasses, neither will your Father forgive your trespasses." Matthew uses debts and sins/trespasses interchangeably. To be forgiven our sins/debts by God, we should first forgive other people's sins/debts before we ask God to forgive our sins/debts. Jesus makes the order of forgiveness clear. Although our relationship with God is more important than with other people, our relationship with other people should be resolved before we try to have a good relationship with God. When we want to be reconciled with God, we should first be reconciled among people (Ephesians 2:14-18).

### Debt of Love

Paul in Romans 13:8-10 says: "[8]Let no debt remain outstanding, except the continuing debt to love one another, for whoever loves others has fulfilled the law. [9]The commandments, "You shall not commit adultery," "You shall not murder," "You shall not steal," "You shall not covet," and whatever other command there may be, are summed up in this one command: "Love your neighbor as yourself." [10]Love does no harm to a neighbor. Therefore, love is the fulfillment of the law" (NIV). Paul considered himself a debtor even after he had confidence that his debts/sins that would lead him to death were all forgiven. What was his remaining debt? Paul felt that he still owed the debt of love to God who had sent Jesus Christ to the world to forgive all people's debts by letting him die on the cross. Jesus appeared in the form of light to Saul/Paul while he was on his way to Damascus to persecute Christians (Acts 9:1-9). When Jesus called Saul/Paul to send him to the Gentiles, he became a debtor of love.

## Chapter Eight

# Wealth, Poverty, and Inequality

### Wealth

Going back to the economy of God, when God created human beings, he blessed them in Genesis 1:28, and again in Genesis 9:1 and 7 he blessed Noah and his sons with the same wording. The Hebrew word, פְּרוּ (pə-rū, from פָּרָה parah) in Genesis 1:28, 9:1 and 7, means "be fruitful," "bear fruit" and occurs 29 times in the Old Testament.[13] The Hebrew word, רְבוּ (rə-bū, from רָבָה (rabah) in Genesis 1:28, 9:1 and 7, means "become many or much," "multiply" and occurs 230 times.[14] God wants his people to be fruitful (or prosper) and multiply in number and in wealth.

God blessed Abraham in Genesis 17:6 and 8: "[6]I will make you exceedingly fruitful; and I will make nations of you, and kings shall come forth from you. … [8]And I will give to you, and to your descendants after you, the land of your sojourning, all the land of Canaan, for an everlasting possession; and I will be their God."; and in 17:20: "… I will bless him(=Ishmael) and make him fruitful and multiply him exceedingly. …" God's blessing of "be fruitful and multiply" includes the blessing of wealth. Abraham's servant in Genesis 24:35 states: "[35]The LORD has greatly blessed my master and he has become great; he has given him flocks and herds, silver and gold, menservants and maidservants, camels and asses." Genesis 26:12-14 states: "[12]Isaac sowed in that land and reaped in the same year a hundredfold. The Lord blessed him, [13]and the man became rich, and gained more and more until he became very wealthy. [14]He had possessions of flocks and herds, and a great household, so that the Philistines envied him." The word "wealthy" is the Hebrew word, גָּדֵל

---

[13] Strong's Hebrew Concordance, "6509. parah," *BibleHub*. Retrieved from https://biblehub.com/hebrew/6509.htm

[14] Ibid., "7235. rabah," *BibleHub*. Retrieved from https://biblehub.com/hebrew/7235.htm

(gadal), which means "great," "become great," "become rich or wealthy."[15] This Hebrew word, גָּדַל (gadal) occurs 115 times in the Old Testament.

God's blessing on Abraham and Isaac was succeeded to his descendants. Isaac blessed Jacob in Genesis 28:3-4: "[3]God Almighty bless you and make you fruitful and multiply you, that you may become a company of peoples. [4]May he give the blessing of Abraham to you and to your descendants with you, that you may take possession of the land of your sojourning which God gave to Abraham!" God said to Jacob in Genesis 35:11-12: "[11]I am God Almighty; be fruitful and increase in number. A nation and a community of nations will come from you, and kings will be among your descendants. [12]The land I gave to Abraham and Isaac I also give to you, and I will give this land to your descendants after you." When we love God and follow his instructions, God's grace and blessings will continue to our children and their children (Exodus 20:6; Deuteronomy 5:10).

Moses in Deuteronomy 8:17-18 tells the Israelites: "[17]Beware lest you say in your heart, 'My power and the might of my hand have gotten me this wealth.' [18]You shall remember the Lord your God, for it is he who gives you power to get wealth; that he may confirm his covenant which he swore to your fathers, as at this day." The word "wealth" here is the Hebrew word, חַ֫יִל (chayil), which means "strength," "wealth," or "army."[16] This Hebrew word, חַ֫יִל (chayil) occurs 224 times in the Old Testament.

### Poverty

Poverty has been a long-discussed issue in our human history. The Scripture also deals with this poverty issue in several different places. Moses in Deuteronomy 15:7-8 states: "If there is among you a poor man, one of your brethren, in any of your towns within your land which the LORD your God gives you, you shall not harden your heart

---

[15] Ibid., "1431. gadal," *BibleHub.* Retrieved from https://biblehub.com/hebrew/1431.htm
[16] Ibid., "2428. chayil," *BibleHub.* Retrieved from https://biblehub.com/hebrew/2428.htm

or shut your hand against your poor brother, but you shall open your hand to him, and lend him sufficient for his need, whatever it may be."

Proverbs 22:22-23 states: "Do not exploit the poor because they are poor and do not crush the needy in court, for the LORD will take up their case and will plunder those who plunder them." God is the God of mercy. He wants us to share what we possess with our poor brothers and sisters, and neighbors.

**Wealth and Poverty as God's Blessing or Curse**

Wealth is considered God's blessing throughout the Bible. However, the Bible also notices that there are some rich people who gathered their wealth in an unlawful or a wicked manner. Poverty may not be God's curse – sometimes, it may be God's blessing when it makes people humble before God. However, there are some people who are poor out of their laziness.

In the following verses, wealth seems to be God's blessing and poverty God's curse:

> Proverbs 8:20-21: "I walk in the way of righteousness, in the paths of justice, endowing with wealth those who love me, and filling their treasuries."
>
> Proverbs 10:4: "A slack hand causes poverty, but the hand of the diligent makes rich."
>
> Proverbs 10:15: "A rich man's wealth is his strong city; the poverty of the poor is their ruin."
>
> Proverbs 19:4: "Wealth brings many new friends, but a poor man is deserted by his friend."
>
> Proverbs 21:5: "The plans of the diligent lead surely to abundance, but everyone who is hasty comes only to want."

Yet, in the following verses, wealth seems to be God's curse and poverty God's blessing:

> Proverbs 15:16: "Better a little with the fear of the LORD than great treasure and trouble with it."

> Proverbs 17:1: "Better is a dry morsel with quiet than a house full of feasting with strife."

Agur in Proverbs 30:7-9 prays to God: "7Two things I ask of thee; deny them not to me before I die: 8Remove far from me falsehood and lying; give me neither poverty nor riches; feed me with the food that is needful for me, 9lest I be full, and deny thee, and say, 'Who is the Lord?' or lest I be poor, and steal, and profane the name of my God." Agur thought that (too much) wealth may not be God's blessing when it makes him deny God and that (too much) poverty may not be God's blessing, either, when it makes him steal and thus dishonor God.

### Wealth and Poverty in the Gospels

In Jesus' saying, wealth does not seem to be God's blessing but may be an obstacle that prevents people from loving God. Jesus in Matthew 6:24 (also in Luke 16:13) says: "No one can serve two masters. Either you will hate the one and love the other, or you will be devoted to the one and despise the other. You cannot serve both God and money." What Jesus tells us here is a matter of choice or priority. We should not choose money over God in any circumstances. Jesus in Luke 14:26 says: "If anyone comes to me and does not hate his father and mother, his wife and children, his brothers and sisters – yes, even his own life – he cannot be my disciple."

In Matthew 19:16ff, a rich young man came to Jesus and asked: "Teacher, what good thing must I do to get eternal life?" (19:16) Jesus' initial answer was a relatively easy one for him: "If you want to get eternal life, obey the commandments." (19:17) The young man inquired: "Which ones?" (19:18a) Jesus replied: "Do not murder, do not commit adultery, do not steal, do not give false testimony, honor your father and mother, and love your neighbor as yourself." (19:18b-19). The young man responded with confidence: "All these I have kept. What do I still lack?" (19:20) Jesus replied: "If you want to be perfect, go, sell your possessions and give to the poor, and you will have treasure in heaven. Then come, follow me." (19:21) When the young man heard this, he went away sad, because he had great wealth." (19:22). Although the rich young man thought that he had kept all the law, he could not give up his wealth (money). Giving up money was much harder than serving God truly. In this sense, this rich young man's wealth was not a God's blessing. After this, Jesus tells his disciples in Matthew 19:23-24: "[23]Truly I tell you, it is hard for someone who is rich to enter the kingdom of heaven. [24]Again I tell you, it is easier for a camel to go through the eye of a needle than for someone who is rich to enter the kingdom of God."

On the other hand, it seems to be easier for the poor people to enter the kingdom of God as poverty makes them humble before God. Jesus in Matthew 5:3 says: "Blessed are the poor in spirit, for theirs is the kingdom of heaven." Not only those who are poor in spirit but also those who are poor in material may be the blessed ones.

Jesus in Luke 6:20-21 says: "[20]Blessed are you who are poor, for yours is the kingdom of God. [21]Blessed are you who hunger now, for you will be satisfied." It may be Luke, who was a physician and thought that "the poor" is not only those who are poor in spirit but also those who are poor in material. That is why he did not include "in spirit" in his writing. Then, you may ask a question: "is it unethical to make big money?"

Jesus in Matthew 25:14ff tells his disciples a parable of the talents. A master called his servants and entrusted his property to them before he departed his house for a journey. To one he gave five talents of money, and to another two talents, and to another one talent, each according to his ability. One talent was equivalent to 5,000-6,000 denarii. And one denarius was equivalent to an average worker's one day pay. So, if we assume an average worker's one day pay is $150, one talent was equivalent to about $800,000. The man who had received the five talents went at once and put his money to work and gained five more. (25:16) So also, the one with the two talents gained two more. (25:17) But the man who had received the one talent went off, dug a hole in the ground and hid his master's money – so, no money was created. (25:18) After a long time, the master returned from his journey and settled accounts with them. (25:19) The man who had received the five talents brought the other five. And he said: "Master, you entrusted me with five talents. See, I have gained five more." (25:20). His master replied: "Well done, good and faithful servant! You have been faithful with a few things; I will put you in charge of many things. Come and share your master's happiness." (25:21) The man with the two talents also came and said: "Master, you entrusted me with two talents; see, I have gained two more." (25:22) His master commended him with the same wording: "Well done, good and faithful servant! You have been faithful with a few things; I will put you in charge of many things. Come and share your master's happiness." (25:23) Then the man who had received the one talent came and said: "Master, I knew that you are a hard man, harvesting where you have not sown and gathering where you have not scattered seed. So I was afraid and went out and hid your talent in the ground. See, here is what belongs to you." (25:24-25) His master replied: "You wicked, lazy servant! So, you knew that I harvest where I have not sown and gather where I have not scattered seed? Well then, you should have put my money on deposit with the bankers, so that when I returned I would have received it back with interest." (25:26-27) The parable of the talents may refer to our faithful work for God and his kingdom. However, it also can be our making money for our daily living, managing our wealth for a better life. Working hard to make more money is nothing wrong if we do honestly and always place God first.

### Love of Money

Most people if not all like or love money. Howard Dayton points out that the Bible contains 2,350 verses that deal with money.[17] What does this mean? Money is so important in our life that we cannot avoid the money matter. Jesus in Luke 16:11 says: "If then you have not been faithful in the unrighteous mammon, who will entrust to you the true riches?" We may need to deal with money properly and faithfully to also deal with more important spiritual matters faithfully. Paul in 1 Timothy 6:10 states: "For the love of money is the root of all evils; it is through this craving that some have wandered away from the faith and pierced their hearts with many pangs." As Jesus states in Matthew 6:24, what Paul says here is a matter of choice or priority. Money

---

[17] Howard Dayton, *Your Money Counts*. Carol Stream, IL: Tyndale House Publishers, Inc., 1996, 4-5.

should not be a Christian's first priority. Money or wealth itself is neutral. However, people's too much greed or too much love of money may cause an ethical problem.

According to John Calvin (1509-1564), the founder of Presbyterianism, money not merely serves for the utilitarian purpose but also functions as the sign of God's grace. Calvin understands money in its twofold meanings: (1) the sign of grace and (2) the sign of condemnation. If a Christian uses money for the good purpose according to God's will, money will be the sign of God's grace. However, if anyone places his/her first priority on (the power of) money, money becomes the sign of condemnation (1 Timothy 6:10).

The 2007-2009 financial crisis was caused not only by the housing market bubble but also more importantly by people's moral hazard problems and/or business people's unethical ways of life. Money or wealth may be important not only to non-Christians but also to Christians as it is critical to everyone's living in this world. However, a Christian worldview is different from a secular worldview as a Christian's priority is God and His kingdom whereas a non-Christian's priority is this world and things that belong to this world such as money.

How many of you do not love money? What is your choice between God and money? Is God always before money in your life and in your decision making? When someone tells you that he will give you $5,000 if you work for him on Sunday (morning to evening), will you decline the offer as you attend church to worship God? Paul's saying in 1 Timothy 6:10 is a challenge that we may encounter in our life as we love money, too. When Abraham was tested by God in Genesis Chapter 20 and was told to offer his only son Isaac as a burnt offering, he could pass the test by giving up his son to choose God. When we choose God over money, we can pass God's test.

## The Poor and the Rich in the Book of James

James 2:5-7 states: "[5]Listen, my beloved brethren. Has not God chosen those who are poor in the world to be rich in faith and heirs of the kingdom which he has promised to those who love him? [6]But you have dishonored the poor man. Is it not the rich who oppress you, is it not they who drag you into court? [7]Is it not they who blaspheme the honorable name which was invoked over you?" As you see in James 2:5-7, James believed that God chose the poor to make them rich in faith and thus to inherit the kingdom of God. The rich have a negative connotation in James. Again, James 5:1-6 warns the rich about the coming judgment.

## Income Inequality

Income inequality is a serious issue in today's society. The gap in wealth or income between the rich and the poor has been widened or cannot be narrowed. Victor Claar and Robin Klay notice that the average worker in the United States has been poorer over time and that the earnings gap between college graduates and high school graduates is becoming wider.[18] This widening of income inequality is not only in the United States but also in many other countries as the modern society uses more technology.

How can the rich and the poor live in harmony as they may be all God's people? Proverbs 22:2 states: "The rich and the poor meet together; the LORD is the maker of them all." How can Christians overcome the issues of poverty and income inequality? The early church Christians shared their possessions with others: "And all who believed were together and had all things in common; and they sold their possessions and goods and distributed them to all, as any had need" (Act 2:44-45); "Now the company of those who believed were of one heart and soul, and no one said that any of the things which he possessed was his own, but they had everything in common" (Acts 4:32). By doing so, income inequality could be reduced or removed among Christians in the early church.

---

[18] Victor V. Claar & Robin J. Klay, *Economics in Christian Perspective: Theory, Policy and Life Choices*, IVP Press, 2007, 194.

Paul also promotes the economy of equality in 2 Corinthians Chapters 8-9 where Paul was campaigning the collection of money for the poor saints in Jerusalem due to a famine. Paul in 2 Corinthians 8:13-14 states: "Our desire is not that others might be relieved while you are hard pressed, but that there might be equality. At the present time your plenty will supply what you need. Then there will be equality." Paul finds his rationale from Exodus 16:16-18, the Israelites' gathering of manna: "This is what the LORD commanded: 'Each one is to gather as much as he needs. Take an omer for each person you have in your tent.' the Israelites did as they were told; some gathered much, some little. And when they measured it by the omer, he who gathered much did not have too much, and he who gathered little did not have too little. Each one gathered as much as he needed." The rich in material has an obligation to share their wealth with the poor in material; the rich in spirit has also an obligation to share their spiritual rich with the poor in spirit. I call this economics of equality.[19]

---

[19] K. P. Choi, *Paul's Life, Epistles, and the Central Themes of His Theology* (in Korean). Seoul, Korea: Qumran Publishing House, 2013, 249-251 & 255-257.

## Chapter Nine

# Communism versus Commonism

### Economic Systems

There are various economic systems that include capitalism, socialism, communism, etc. Capitalism tries to follow the market economy that determines the price and quantity in the market whereas socialism the central economy that the price and quantity are determined by a central authority. Most countries in capitalism may not follow the market economy but the mixed economy in which the market usually determines the price and quantity, but sometimes the government intervenes in the market to regulate the price and/or the quantity.

### Capitalism

Capitalism is an economic system characterized by private ownership of resources and markets, which is also called the free enterprise system. [20] Another important characteristic of capitalism is decentralized decision making, using markets. No nation in the world precisely fits the two criteria for capitalism; however, the United States comes close. The strengths of capitalism include its capacity to achieve economic efficiency because competition and the profit motive force production at the lowest cost, and economic freedom because economic power is widely dispersed. The weaknesses of capitalism include capitalism tends toward an unequal distribution of income; private markets can fail to provide an adequate amount of public goods; capitalism inevitably leads to macroeconomic instability that can result in severe recessions or even depressions; and capitalism fails to protect the environment.

---

[20] Irvin B. Tucker, *Economics for Today* (10th ed.). Cengage Learning, 2019, 794-795.

## Socialism

Socialism is an economic system characterized by government ownership of resources and centralized decision making. [21] Its characteristics are public/government ownership and centralization. Under a socialist economy, a command system owns and controls in the public interest the major industries, such as steel, electricity, and agriculture. However, some free markets can exist in farming, retail trade, and certain service areas. The market failures in a capitalist system create so much economic hardship that a country is better off using socialism to organize its production. However, the government may fail to improve on these market outcomes. Or worse yet, government intervention may make matters worse. Socialism produces poor economic results mostly because some government officials are corrupt, ignorant, or succumb to special-interest-group political pressure. The strengths of socialism include: There is an equitable distribution of income because government ownership of capital and other resources prevents a few individuals or groups from acquiring a disproportionate share of the nation's wealth; rapid economic growth is achieved when planners have the power to direct more resources to producing capital goods and fewer resources to producing consumer goods; and there is no unemployment. The weaknesses of socialism include: Economic inefficiency results because the government often uses many workers to perform work that requires only one or two workers; the absence of the profit motive discourages entrepreneurship and innovation and thus suppresses economic growth; the central planning process is subject to errors and is unresponsive to the wants of the majority of the population; and "perks" for government officials, nepotism, and the illegal use of markets create disparities in income.

## Communism

Karl Marx rejected capitalism and saw profits as unjust payments to owners of firms – the capitalists. Marx believed that the market system would destroy itself because wealthy owners would go too far and exploit workers as unrelenting greed for profits would lead the owners

---

[21] Ibid., 795-796.

to pay starvation wages. Marx thought that private ownership and exploitation would produce a nation driven by a class struggle between a few "haves" and many "have-nots." Marx believed communism to be the ideal system.

Communism is a stateless, classless economic system in which all the factors of production are owned by the workers (common ownership, no private property), and people share production according to their needs.[22] In ideal communism, each worker produces according to his/her ability and consumes according his/her needs. Free access to the items of consumption is made possible by advances in technology that allow for super-abundance.[23] In Marx's view, this is the highest form of socialism toward which the revolution should strive. No nation has achieved the ideal communist society described by Marx, or has capitalism self-destructed as he predicted.

## Communism versus Socialism

Many countries have socialist political parties and economic system, but very few (or none) have a truly communistic economic system. Many countries have government programs that borrow from socialist principles. Socialism is frequently interchangeably used with communism, but the two economic systems or ideologies have differences.[24] In socialism properties are owned by the central authority or the government whereas in communism properties are owned commonly by all workers. In socialism the central authority or the government has strong power whereas in ideal communism no state exists.

## Commonism

The early church Christians shared their possessions with others: "All the believers were together and had everything in common. Selling their possessions and goods, they gave to anyone as he had need" (Acts 2:44-45); "All the believers were one in heart and mind. No one

[22] Ibid., 796-797.

[23] Anonymous, "Communism vs. Socialism," *Diffen*. Retrieved from https://www.diffen.com/difference/Communism_vs_Socialism

[24] Ibid.

claimed that any of his possessions was his own, but they shared everything they had" (Acts 4:32). The early church Christians' life within a Christian community, which I call 'commonism,' was very similar to an ideal life in communism. People could use/consume items as they needed. However, there is no private ownership granted but common ownership in communism whereas there was private ownership in commonism although people did not claim private ownership once they brought their possessions to the church/community. The early church Christians believed that they were one body of Christ, who is the head of the (universal or catholic) church and lived a life for others as they were the branches of the same body. The early church's commonism (or commonal life) was according to the economic principle of sharing or equality.

As we examined, in capitalism individuals make money according to their ability and spend it as they want. A primary problem with capitalism is that it widens income inequality – the rich may become richer, the poor poorer. The inequality gap cannot be narrowed, and this has been one of the most serious issues in today's capitalist countries.

In communism individuals work using the production tools that are commonly possessed and spend as they need. In communism all are owned by workers/individuals commonly or collectively. Communism seems to be ideal, but this common ownership reduces overachievers' desire or incentive to work hard as people are selfish or individualistic that they want to possess their own property by nature. Thus, communism lowers productivity of the economy as a whole and may lead the society to poverty.

However, a society in commonism is fundamentally different from a society in communism. Commonism does not deny or reject the strengths of capitalism but it complements its weaknesses. That is, in commonism individuals make money according to their ability like in capitalism. People possess their own property/wealth. However, they are willing to share their possession with poorer people by bringing some or whole of them to the community or church (this is a voluntary sharing not a forced sharing by the government or the central authority), believing that their poorer neighbors are the branches of the same body and loving them.[25]

## The Origin of Commonism

This spirit of commonism is from Jesus' teaching of sharing. Jesus in Matthew 14:13-21 (also in Mark 6:30-44; Luke 9:10-17; and John 6:1-14) fed five thousand men (not counting women and children). If Jesus had not taken a boy's five loaves and two fish and shared them, those people who gathered would have suffered from hunger and those five loaves of bread and two fish could have been only one boy's lunch meal. But when Jesus took and broke them, the crowd with his disciples could see the miracle of abundant feeding, with remaining of twelve baskets full. Jesus let his disciples partake in this miraculous feeding, telling them, "<u>You</u> give them (the crowd) something to eat." (Matthew 14:16). And Matthew 14:19 states: "Then he ordered the crowds to sit down on the grass; and taking the five loaves and the two fish he looked up to heaven, and blessed, and broke and gave the loaves to the disciples, and the disciples gave them to the crowds." Jesus' disciples were partakers of this miracle.

Jesus in Matthew 25:31-46 speaks about the judgment of the nations. When the Son of Man comes in his glory, he will separate people one from another as a shepherd separates the sheep from the goat. Then the king (Son of Man) will say to the people on his right in Matthew 25:34-36: "[34]Come, O blessed of my Father, inherit the kingdom prepared for you from the foundation of the world; [35]for I was hungry and you gave me food, I was thirsty and you gave me drink, I was a stranger and you welcomed me, [36]I was naked and you clothed me, I was sick and you visited me, I was in prison and you came to me."

What Jesus fed the crowd (Matthew 14:13-21, 16:5-12) and told his disciples about the judgment of the people (Matthew 25:31-46) was to teach about economic principles of commonism or sharing. What was the problem of the rich young man who visited Jesus in Matthew 19:16-22? He was not willing to share his wealth with the poor

[25] K. P. Choi, *Paul's Life, Epistles, and the Central Themes of His Theology* (in Korean). Seoul, Korea: Qumran Publishing House, 2013, 258-259.

(Matthew 19:21-22). Jesus' teaching of sharing and the commonal life of the early Christians in their community were succeeded by Paul in his economics of sharing, which we will discuss in the next chapter, Chapter 10.

## Chapter Ten

# Economics of Equality

### Entrusted Ownership

As we studied earlier, God had created the heavens and earth, and thus he owns everything in the universe. Then, what about people's private ownership that the Bible states? It is the ownership that God grants them while people live in this world. I call it 'an entrusted ownership,' and Steve Elwart calls it 'a delegated ownership.'[26] As our possessions that we seem to own are not ours, they should be used according to the real owner's will.

What is the will of God toward his people who had been created according to his image and his likeness? God wants each one of his people to "be fruitful, increase in number, and fill the earth" (Genesis 1:28). On their path of life some become richer whereas some others become poorer. What does God want the richer to do for the poorer?

### Collection for the Poor

There are various evidences of the charitable provisions of the relief for the poor in the Old Testament (Exodus 23:10-13; Leviticus 19:9-10, 23:22; Deuteronomy 14:28-29, 15:1-11, 24:19-22). God in Exodus 23:10-11 through Moses states: "[10]For six years you shall sow your land and gather in its yield; [11]but the seventh year you shall let it rest and lie fallow, that the poor of your people may eat; and what they leave the wild beasts may eat. You shall do likewise with your vineyard, and with your olive orchard"; and in Deuteronomy 14:28-29: "[14]At the end of every three years you shall bring forth all the tithe of your produce in the same year, and lay it up within your towns; [29]and the Levite, because he has no portion or inheritance with you, and the sojourner, the fatherless, and the widow, who are within your towns, shall come and

[26] S. Elwart, "Biblical Principles of Economics," *Koinonia House* (October 1, 2011). Retrieved from https://www.khouse.org/articles/2011/1015/

eat and be filled; that the Lord your God may bless you in all the work of your hands that you do." God wants the richer to take care of the poorer by using the land and tithes.

According to K. Nickle, "by the first century A.D. the legislation of charity for the poor had been extended to the local communities": the people in the community were required to pay a tax for the basket collection; and the poor residents "received enough funds to provide two meals a day for the next week."[27] This may be the origin of the basket collection of our church today.

We can also find another earlier instance of the disciples' sending material aid to brothers and sisters in need in Acts 11:27-30. When a severe famine took place over all the world during the reign of Claudius (v. 28), "[29]the disciples determined, everyone according to his ability, to send relief to the brethren who lived in Judea; [30]and they did so, sending it to the elders by the hand of Barnabas and Saul (i.e., Paul)." So, Paul was a member of the delegation of the early church. This might be a good experience for Paul to do it again in the later incidence under his leadership.

## Paul's Collection Campaign

Paul deals with his collection campaign for the poor saints in Jerusalem in his major four epistles, Romans 15:25-28, 1 Corinthians 16:1-4, 2 Corinthians 8-9, and Galatians 2:9-10. Some of the Jewish Christians living at Jerusalem were poverty-stricken whether they deliberately chose to live in that way or not. But Paul had a conviction that the collection for the Jerusalem saints would not only help them financially but also bring all Christian churches who participated in collection into the unity in Jesus Christ. He believed that the spiritual benefits derived from the collection campaign by the givers would far surpass the monetary value of the gift itself. Throughout this campaign, Paul probably would wish to see the reunion and reconciliation of Christians who were going in different directions under different leaderships and beliefs. Paul did not request any money for his own living to the churches that he had founded, but he did tent making to

---

[27] K. F. Nickle, *The Collection: A Study in Paul's Strategy*. Alec R. Allenson Inc., 1966, 93-94.

be self-sufficient. However, he was very active and enthusiastic in doing the collection campaign for the poor people in Jerusalem, sending letters and people to the local churches in Asia Minor, Macedonia, and Achaia.

Paul's love for his fellow Jews was not reduced as we can read in Romans 9-11 although they rejected him and gave difficulties to him. According to Acts, Paul took (at least) three missionary journeys (Acts 13:1-14:28, 15:36-18:22, & 18:23-21:14) throughout his life. The purpose of Paul's third missionary journey was that Paul would collect money from the churches that he had founded and give it to the poor people in Jerusalem, who were suffering from a severe famine. Paul lived a rich spiritual life in the midst of material poverty and obstacles as Jesus did so.

Paul in 2 Corinthians 8-9 asked the people in the church at Corinth to complete their collection that they promised a year before and now is delayed. Paul took a good example of the people in the churches at Macedonia, who were much poorer than the people in the church at Corinth and yet were very much willing to participate in the collection campaign out of their mind of love and could complete it already although they started the collection later than the people in the church at Corinth.

Paul in 2 Corinthians 8:1-5 states: "[1]And now, brothers and sisters, we want you to know about the grace that God has given the Macedonian churches. [2]In the midst of a very severe trial, their overflowing joy and their extreme poverty welled up in rich generosity. [3]For I testify that they gave as much as they were able, and even beyond their ability. Entirely on their own, [4]they urgently pleaded with us for the privilege of sharing in this service to the Lord's people. [5]And they exceeded our expectations: They gave themselves <u>first</u> of all to the Lord, and <u>then</u> by the will of God also to us." Although Paul praises the virtue (gift) of the Macedonians, he attributes their virtue to the grace of God: The Macedonian gift or generosity (8:2-5) comes from the grace of God (8:1).[28] Based on a theological use of χάρις (*charis*, grace or generosity)

---

[28] K. P. Choi, *When I Am Weak, Then I Am Strong: Oikonomia Bible Interpretation Series – 2 Corinthians* (in Korean). Seoul, Korea: Qumran Publishing House, 2001, 221-223.

in 8:1 and an anthropological one in 8:4, C. K. Barrett suggests the two possibilities: (1) "the generosity of the Macedonians is the generosity of God himself"; or (2) "God has given grace to the Macedonians with the result of making them generous."[29] The second one seems to serve better in the passage, but the first one is also plausible. Their generosity in 8:2 is valuable especially because they offered themselves out of their poverty and affliction. Their giving was voluntary as well as cheerful and generous even beyond their means (8:3).

Paul in 2 Corinthians 8:9 states: "For you know the grace of our Lord Jesus Christ, that though he was rich, yet for your sake he became poor, so that you through his poverty might become rich." Paul's economics of equality or sharing follows the example of Jesus' own life. Jesus Christ was rich in the kingdom of God, possessing all the universe and things in it but came down to the earth to live a poor life to make his people who were poor become rich in him. Jesus came down to us, wearing clothes of poverty, to let us who were poor in spirit or in material hear the good news and receive the light of God's grace. Paul asked the Corinthians the same thing by which the poor saints in Jerusalem might be provided. Although our material possession may stay the same before and after we accepted Jesus Christ, we may be said to be rich, in a sense, if we can afford to give ourselves generously for others like the Macedonians in 2 Corinthians 8:1-5. The Macedonians' example in 8:1-5 can be compared with the example of Jesus Christ in 8:9. My summary of the important parallels is in the following table:

| The Macedonians' Example (8:1-5) | The Example of Jesus Christ (8:9) |
|---|---|
| The grace of God (v. 1)<br><br>During a severe ordeal of affliction | The grace (generous act) of our Lord<br><br>(In) the sufferings of Christ |

[29] C. K. Barrett, *A Commentary on the Second Epistle to the Corinthians*, Harper & Row, 1973, 218.

| | |
|---|---|
| (v. 2)<br><br>They **voluntarily** gave (v. 3)<br><br>Out of love for fellow Christians<br><br>(ministry to the saints, v. 4)<br><br>They gave **themselves** (v. 5)<br><br>They became poor so that the saints in Jerusalem might become rich<br><br>Salvific/gracious work[30]<br><br>(salvation of the saints) | (on the cross) (2 Corinthians 1:5)<br><br>Jesus Christ **voluntarily** gave<br><br>Out of love for all human beings<br><br>(ministry to the world)<br><br>Jesus Christ gave **himself**<br><br>Jesus Christ became poor so that we might become rich<br><br>Salvific/gracious work<br><br>(salvation of human beings) |

Note: The NRSV version is used for the table.

Paul in 2 Corinthians 8:12 states: "For if the willingness is there, the gift is acceptable according to what one has, not according to what one does not have." Paul appealed to the Corinthians' eagerness to complete the collection not according to what they do not have but according to what they have. When you share what you have with others, your willingness (out of the mind of love for neighbors) is very important. Furthermore, God does not want you to borrow money to help people in poverty. Your sharing with others is according to what you have, not adding debt.[31]

Paul in 2 Corinthians 8:13-15 explains about the economics of equality or fairness (ἰσότης, isotés): "[13]I do not mean that others should be eased and you burdened, [14]but that as a matter of equality your abundance at the present time should supply their want, so that their abundance may supply your want, that there may be equality. [15]As it is

[30] According to Foerster, "in Paul, χάρις is a central concept that most clearly expresses his understanding of the salvation event." *TDNT*, vol. 9, 1974, 393.
[31] K. P. Choi, *When I Am Weak, Then I Am Strong: Oikonomia Bible Interpretation Series – 2 Corinthians* (in Korean). Seoul, Korea: Qumran Publishing House, 2001, 234.

written: 'He who gathered much had nothing over, and he who gathered little had no lack.'" What Paul asked the Corinthians is a fair balance or equality (ἰσότης, isotés) between their present abundance and the poor saints' need.[32] This kind of material sharing of people in Achaia and Macedonia with the poor saints in Jerusalem seems to be quite fair for Paul who says: "indeed they (the Christians in Achaia and Macedonia) are in debt to them (the poor saints in Jerusalem), for if the Gentiles have come to share in their spiritual blessings, they ought also to be of service to them in material blessings" in Romans 15:27. The verse 14b, "so that their abundance may supply your want, that there may be equality," may be interpreted in two ways. First, as the poor saints in Jerusalem share their spiritual blessings with the Gentiles, so should the Gentiles share their material blessings with the saints (cf. Romans 15:27). Second, when the Gentiles share their material blessings with the Jews now, then someday later, the Jews will share their material (or spiritual) blessings with the Gentiles.[33] Then, there may be "equality" (RSV, NIV, NLT) or "a fair balance" (NRSV).

## Economics of Equality

According to Paul, the economics of equality is to share our current plenty with those who are now in poverty. Then, in some other times, those who receive our plenty now will share their plenty with us who may be in poverty in the future, whatever their plenty is. Paul does not mean that you should be in debt when you help other people financially but that you are willing to share what you have now (no matter how big or small that is) with others.

The ground of Paul's economics of equality also goes back to Exodus 16:18 (see 2 Corinthians 8:15). God told the Israelites through Moses to gather manna as much as they could eat. Some gathered more, some others gathered less (Exodus 16:16-17). Exodus 16:18 states: "But when they measured it with an omer, he that gathered much had

---

[32] Ibid., 235.

[33] Barrett states that Paul "appears to mean only that if in the future there is need in Corinth, the Jerusalem Christians, if they are better off, will share with their Gentile brothers" (p. 226). He seems to exclude the possibility of the first way of interpretation, but I think that it is a possible interpretation from Romans 15:27 for equality or a fair balance.

nothing over, and he that gathered little had no lack; each gathered according to what he could eat." God wants his people to possess neither too much nor too little but equality among them. Moses told the Israelites not to leave any of it till the morning, but some left the part of it and it bred worms and became foul (Exodus 16:19-20).

Paul in 1 Corinthians 9:11-12 states: "[11]If we have sown spiritual good among you, is it too much if we reap your material benefits? [12]If others share this rightful claim upon you, do not we still more? Nevertheless, we have not made use of this right, but we endure anything rather than put an obstacle in the way of the gospel of Christ." When Paul and his coworkers taught the good news (=spiritual plenty) to people in the church at Corinth, Paul thinks that he and his coworkers have a right to be financially helped by them although Paul never claimed his right to be financially helped by the people in the church as Corinth.[34] Instead, Paul wants to ask the people in the church at Corinth to financially help the poor saints in Jerusalem as they are debtors to them. That is, the people in the church at Corinth, the Gentiles, were receivers of spiritual plenty from Jesus Christ and Paul, who were born as Jews. As the people in the church at Corinth were debtors of love of Christ and the gospel when they became Christians in the past, it seems to be obvious that they should share their material plenty with the poor Jews in Jerusalem who are suffering from the great famine now.

Paul in Romans 15:25-27 describes his third missionary journey in which he is heading for Jerusalem: "[25]At present, however, I am going to Jerusalem with aid for the saints. [26]For Macedonia and Achaia have been pleased to make some contribution for the poor among the saints at Jerusalem; [27]they were pleased to do it, and indeed they are in debt to them, for if the Gentiles have come to share in their spiritual blessings, they ought also to be of service to them in material blessings." Again, this is the basic principle of Paul's economics of equality.[35] Whenever you have something plenty now, you are willing to share it

---

[34] K. P. Choi, *Except Jesus Christ and Him Crucified: Oikonomia Bible Interpretation Series 4 – 1 Corinthians* (in Korean). Seoul, Korea: Qumran Publishing House, 2000, 238.

[35] K. P. Choi, *Present Your Bodies as a Living Sacrifice: Oikonomia Bible Interpretation Series 1 – Romans* (in Korean). Seoul, Korea: Qumran Publishing House, 1999, 318-322.

with others who lack it; then, whenever others who lack the one that you have now will share their plenty with you who will lack it in the future. It does not matter whatever that is – it may be material plenty (money, time, land, labor, etc.) or spiritual plenty (love, grace, gospel, etc.).

From the Old Testament to the New Testament, God wants his people to prosper, multiply, and fill the earth. Some become wealthy whereas some others become poor. God wants the richer to share their wealth with the poorer. God wants to feed each one of his people and see each one of them be satisfied and gives thanks to God with a humble mind, acknowledging that God is his/her LORD and Master.

Jesus Christ had come to us, wearing the clothes of poverty although he was rich, to make us become rich by his poverty. Jesus Christ had died on the cross, being cursed (Gal. 3:13), so that we may live eternally, being blessed. Paul in Galatians 3:13 states: "Christ redeemed us from the curse of the law, having become a curse for us – for it is written, 'Cursed be everyone who hangs on a tree'." Jesus Christ fed his people – his disciples and the crowd who followed him – and taught them to share among themselves. Paul succeeded Jesus' teaching of sharing and taught the economics of equality between the Jews and the Gentiles, between male and female, and between the masters and the slaves.

Paul in Galatians 3:26-29 emphasizes equality or oneness in Christ: "[26]for in Christ Jesus you are all sons of God, through faith. [27]For as many of you as were baptized into Christ have put on Christ. [28]There is neither Jew nor Greek, there is neither slave nor free, there is neither male nor female; for you are all one (or equal) in Christ Jesus. [29]And if you are Christ's, then you are Abraham's offspring, heirs according to promise." Paul in Ephesians 2:14-16 states, emphasizing oneness (or equality) in Christ: "[14]For he is our peace, who has made us both one, and has broken down the dividing wall of hostility, [15]by abolishing in his flesh the law of commandments and ordinances, that he might create in himself one new man in place of the two, so making peace, [16]and might reconcile us both to God in one body through the cross, thereby bringing the hostility to an end." Paul's economics of equality is not limited only to material matters but can be expanded to every aspect of our life in Christ despite our differences in race/ethnicity, sex, class, wealth, age, etc.

John Calvin, succeeding Paul's economics of equality, states that the rich is called to share their material wealth with the poor (a providential economic mission to fulfill) whereas the poor is called to share their spiritual wealth with the rich (a providential spiritual mission to fulfill) by God (cf. 2 Corinthians 8:14). Thus, the rich are the ministers/servants of God to the poor, and the poor are the vicars of Christ to the rich.

# PART II

# THE ECONOMY OF A HOUSEHOLD:

# MICROECONOMC ASPECTS

# Chapter Eleven

# What Is the Economy of a Household?

Up until now, we studied about the economy of God – God's governing activities and instructions for his household as a whole, which is a macroeconomic aspect. Today, we expect that the economy of God – God's governing activities – is entrusted to the government. Now, we will move to each individual's or individual household's economy, that is, decision making for himself/herself or his/her household, which is the microeconomic aspect of our study.

## Maximization of Satisfaction

In economics each individual's economic goal is to maximize his/her utility – satisfaction or happiness – as a consumer or to maximize profit as a business owner. As we examined, the first meaning of an economy (*oikonomia*) is "stewardship or the management of a household." Each individual as a manager of a household, whether he/she is a consumer or business owner, he/she wants to maximize satisfaction for himself/herself and for his/her household. How can an individual maximize his/her satisfaction in his/her economic activities? What are economic activities? In economics a person's economic activities are his/her decision making in his/her daily life – in his/her consumer behavior and/or producer behavior. An individual's satisfaction may be larger when he/she makes more money for his/her consumption or from his/her production or business. Like non-Christians, Christian households/consumers want to maximize their utility and Christian firms/producers want to maximize their profit. However, the ways and/or the methods that they maximize their utility/satisfaction or profit are different from those of non-Christians as God is at the center of their life. That is, by pleasing God and following the command of Jesus Christ, Christian households/consumers can maximize their utility/satisfaction and Christian firms/producers can maximize their profit.

What about us as a Christian? A Christian's satisfaction can be maximized when he/she has a good relationship with God. A Christian as a steward takes care of a household that God entrusts to him/her. That is, a Christian takes care of his/her household that belongs to the household of God.

## Stewardship

Hugh Whelchel in his article, "Four Principles of Biblical Stewardship," lists 1. the principle of ownership, 2. the principle of responsibility, 3. the principle of accountability, and 4. the principle of reward.[36] Whelchel's four principles make sense when we acknowledge that all things belong to God and our job on this earth is to take a good care of a small portion of God's that is entrusted to us while we live here in this world. That is, acknowledgement of God's ownership of everything is the starting point of a Christian's stewardship or management of (a small unit of) his household. God placed Adam in the Garden of Eden and let him work and take care of it (Genesis 2:15). God considered Adam as a steward or a manager of his garden or household.

God tells the Israelites through Moses in Leviticus 25:23-24: "[23]The land must never be sold on a permanent basis, for the land belongs to me. You are only foreigners and tenant farmers working for me. [24]With every purchase of land you must grant the seller the right to buy it back" (NLT). Although many people think that they own the land, the house or household, or money, all these belong to God and we are his stewards working for him and our duty is stewardship for God's household. We can find many more Bible verses regarding God's ownership and our temporary possession as his stewards or tenants.

Moses tells the Israelites in Deuteronomy 10:14: "To the Lord your God belong the heavens, even the highest heavens, the earth and everything in it." Psalm 24:1-2 states: "[1]The earth is the Lord's, and everything in it, the world, and all who live in it; [2]for he founded it on the seas and established it on the waters." When God calls his people

---

[36] Hugh Whelchel, "Four Principles of Biblical Stewardship," *Institute for Faith, Work, & Economics.* (November 26, 2012). Retrieved from https://tifwe.org/four-principles-of-biblical-stewardship/

– Enoch (Genesis 5:22), Noah (Genesis 6:13), Abraham (Genesis 12:1-3), Moses (Exodus 3:4ff.) and the Israelites, and others, each one of God's people starts his life as a steward or a manager of his household, separating himself from the secular world and acknowledging God's ownership and also our delegated ownership.

Moses in Deuteronomy 8:17-18 reminded the Israelites of this fact: "[17]You may say to yourself, 'My power and the strength of my hands have produced this wealth for me.' [18]But remember the Lord your God, for it is he who gives you the ability to produce wealth, and so confirms his covenant, which he swore to your ancestors, as it is today." Yes, it is God's grace that we produce wealth and increase it, but we know that all things belong to God and we are his stewards who manage his properties until we meet him for accounting.

David in 1 Chronicles 29:14 says to God: "But who am I, and who are my people, that we should be able to give as generously as this? Everything comes from you, and we have given you only what comes from your hand." Although some may think they offer their money to God, they should recognize that they give what God allows them to possess (as everything comes from God).

## Management of God's Household

Jesus in Luke 16:2-4 tells a parable of a shrewd steward: "[2]And he (a rich man) called him (a steward) and said to him, 'What is this that I hear about you? Turn in the account of your stewardship, for you can no longer be steward.' [3]And the steward said to himself, 'What shall I do, since my master is taking the stewardship away from me? I am not strong enough to dig, and I am ashamed to beg. [4]I have decided what to do, so that people may receive me into their houses when I am put out of the stewardship.'" In this Jesus' parable of the shrewd (or wicked) manager, the master commended his dishonest steward because he acted shrewdly although he was accused of wasting his possessions (v. 8). However, his dishonesty or wickedness cannot be justified. What Jesus emphasizes here is not that God's steward can be dishonest if he/she acts shrewdly but that God's steward should be more shrewd and wiser than the worldly manager in managing the household of God.

Jesus in Luke 16:10-12 says: "[10]Whoever can be trusted with very little can also be trusted with much, and whoever is dishonest with very little will also be dishonest with much. [11]So if you have not been trustworthy (πιστοὶ from πιστός) in handling worldly wealth, who will (en)trust (πιστεύσει from πιστεύω) you with true riches? [12]And if you have not been trustworthy (πιστοὶ from πιστός) with someone else's property, who will give you property of your own?" We as a manager of God's property or household should be trustworthy (πιστός). Then, later, in God's kingdom, God may give us property of our own. Paul in 1 Corinthians 4:1-2 states: "[1]This is how one should regard us, as servants of Christ and stewards of the mysteries of God. [2]Moreover it is required of stewards that they be found trustworthy (πιστός)." Although our ownership in this world is not a true ownership but an entrusted or delegated ownership but our ownership in God's kingdom will be our real ownership.

In Jesus' parable of the talents (Matthew 25:14-30), the servants who received different talents would not consider that the master gave the talents to them but that he entrusted his property (talents) to them and let them manage the talents while he was going on a journey (Matthew 25:14). However, the master who returned from his long journey (which implies Jesus' second coming) did not collect the talents from his servants but let them have them – the initial talents and the earnings. Jesus in Matthew 25:28-29 says: "[28]So take the talent from him and give it to him who has (owns) the ten talents. [29]For to everyone who has (owns) will more be given, and he will have abundance; but from him who has not, even what he has will be taken away."

God gives spiritual gifts to his people (Romans 12:6-8; 1 Corinthians 12-13; Ephesians 4:11; and 1 Peter 4:11), letting them manage God's household more effectively and wisely. However, some people boast about their spiritual gifts without knowing the true purpose of spiritual gifts. No matter what (wealth, land, spiritual gifts, or other things, etc.) God entrusts us, God's will toward us is to take a good care of his household.

## Chapter Twelve

# A Steward or a Manager of a Household

### God's Initial Call of People

Hugh Whelchel states that Genesis 1:28 is the original call (of human beings) to stewardship.[37] God wanted first human beings to "be fruitful and multiply and fill the earth," for which God created and called them. Then, this calling for blessing reappears several times (Genesis 9:1 & 9, 17:6 & 20, 28:3, 35:11) as we examined in Chapter 9. While God blessed Adam, he placed him in the Garden of Eden as his steward to work and take care of his garden (Genesis 2:15) until Adam and Eve fell. God wanted Adam and Eve to be faithful or trustworthy in their stewardship and live there freely with their free will as long as they would not eat the fruit from the tree of the knowledge of good and evil.

### A Steward in the Old Testament

A steward is different from a slave as a steward has freedom of decision making whereas a slave is only to behave according to what his master dictates him/her. Genesis 15:2 states: "And Abram said, 'Lord God, what wilt thou give me, seeing I go childless, and the steward of my house is this Eliezer of Damascus?'" (KJV). Eliezer was Abraham's faithful servant whom Abraham called here 'the steward' (מֶשֶׁק, mesheq), which is also translated as 'heir' (RSV). The Hebrew word, מֶשֶׁק (mesheq), etymologically means 'acquisition' or 'possession' although its root is not quite certain.[38]

---

[37] Ibid., "Three Key Passages Concerning Stewardship in the Bible," *Institute for Faith, Work & Economics.* (October 19, 2016). Retrieved from https://tifwe.org/stewardship-in-the-bible.

[38] Strong's Hebrew Concordance, "4943. mesheq," *BibleHub.* Retrieved from https://biblehub.com/hebrew/4943.htm.

**A Steward in the New Testament**

The Greek word, "οἰκονόμος (oikonomos)" – a compound word of οἶκος (oikos, house or household) and νέμω (nemō, manage or dispense) – corresponds to the English word, 'a steward' or 'a household manager.' This makes sense as we Christians are not the real owner or master of our household but a delegated owner or a manager to whom God's property is entrusted to take care of a small unit of God's household.

Jesus in Luke 12:42-44 says: "[42]Who then is the faithful and wise steward, whom his master will set over his household, to give them their portion of food at the proper time? [43]Blessed is that servant whom his master when he comes will find so doing. [44]Truly, I say to you, he will set him over all his possessions." The steward in this Jesus' parable takes care of people in his household (other servants or slaves) as well as all his possessions. The steward (or manager) should be responsible and accountable as he should take care of his master's household, including his people and wealth. Jesus in Luke 12:48 says: "Everyone to whom much is given, of him will much be required; and of him to whom men commit much they will demand the more."

In Jesus' parable of the shrewd or wicked steward in Luke 16:1-13, the steward was accused of his master's possessions. The master entrusted his possessions to his steward and let him manage them according to his ability but did not want him to waste them but make more profit for him. Jesus in Luke 16:13 says: "No servant can serve two masters; for either he will hate the one and love the other, or he will be devoted to the one and despise the other. You cannot serve God and mammon (=money)." As a steward of a household we may possess or deal with (master's) money. But Jesus warns us that we cannot serve both God and money. This is a matter of priority – we should not place money before God.

Jesus in Luke 19:11-27 tells us the parable of ten minas (or pounds), which is similar to the parable of talents in Matthew 25:14-30. This parable seems to be a modification of the parable of talents as it is incomplete. A nobleman called ten of his servants and gave them ten minas (one mina per servant) before he went to a distant country (the kingdom of God) to become a king and then to return. One mina (or one pound) was about three months' wages for an average worker. So, one mina is about $12,000-$15,000 in today's value. The master wants each of the servants to do business with the money until he comes back (as an entrepreneur). When he returned as king, he called the ten servants to find out what they had gained with his money (Luke 19:15). Only three servants (out of ten), like in Matthew 25:14-30, appear in the passage. The first servant tells him that he gained ten more minas. The master commends him and gives him authority over ten cities. The second servant tells him that he gained five more minas. The master commends him and gives him authority over five cities. The third servant tells him that he kept the mina laid away in a piece of cloth. The master rebukes him, saying, "[22]I will condemn you out of your own mouth, you wicked servant! You knew that I was a severe man, taking up what I did not lay down and reaping what I did not sow? [23]Why then did you not put my money into the bank, and at my coming I should have collected it with interest?" (Luke 19:22-23). The master tells those standing by to take his mina away from him and give it to the one who had gained ten more minas and says: "I tell you, that to everyone who has will more be given; but from him who has not, even what he has will be taken away" (Luke 19:26). In this parable, unlike in Matthew 25:14-30, every servant was given the equal amount of money (1 mina), and thus there is no issue of unfairness, jealousy, or hatred. So, the third servant's laziness cannot be excused. He simply did not do anything out of his disobedience, unfaithfulness, and laziness.

Jesus' similar but more famous parable of talents is in Matthew 25:14-30. The situation is similar to that of Luke 19:11-27. The master entrusts the different amount of talents to three servants according to their ability. Which one is fair distribution between one mina per servant in Luke 19:11-27 and the different amount of talents according to their ability in Matthew 25:14-30? It may be debatable, but we can see different God-given talents/gifts among us. We may not be able to say it is unfair although we are allowed less God-given talents as it is probably the will of God who knows each one of us better than we know ourselves. We as a steward of his household should not complain about the amount of God-given talents/gifts that we have but should be faithful in managing them. The master in Matthew 25:14-30 gives five talents to one servant, two talents to another servant, and one talent to the third servant. One talent was about 5,000-6,000 denarii, and one denarius was an average worker's one day pay. So, one talent is an average worker's 20-year pay or about $1 million in today's value. After a long time, the master returned and settled accounts with them. The first servant tells him that he gained five more talents. The master commends him, saying, "Well done, good and faithful servant; you have been faithful over a little, I will set you over much; enter into the joy of your master" (Matthew 25:21). The second servant tells him that he gained two more talents. The master commends him, saying, "Well done, good and faithful servant; you have been faithful over a little, I will set you over much; enter into the joy of your master" (Matthew 25:23). The master commends the two servants with the exactly same wording, which is different from Luke 19:11-27. The third servant tells him that he hid the talent in the ground. The master rebukes him, saying, "[26]You wicked and slothful servant! You knew that I reap where I have not sowed, and gather where I have not winnowed? [27]Then you ought to have invested my money with the bankers, and at my coming I should have received what was my own with interest" (Matthew 25:26-27). The master tells those standing by to take the talent from him and give it to the one who has ten talents and says: "For to everyone who has will more be given, and he will have abundance" (Matthew 25:29). God wants each one of his stewards to do his/her best in doing business with the God-given talents/gifts.

When the master gave money to his servants in Luke 19:11-27 and Matthew 25:14-30, he did not tell them what exactly they should do but told them to do a business or put the money to work. The servants were free to do whatever they planned. In this sense, they were entrepreneurs who could start and run their business using their resources (money and labor) and creative ideas. In the same manner, God allows us to do whatever we plan and desire. We are entrepreneurs in our own fields or areas, exercising our constructive ideas, making good use of our resources – labor, human capital, and others. We do our best in running our work for God, using the God-given talents/gifts so that we can maximize profit for God, whatever profit that is.

Paul in 1 Corinthians 4:1-2 states: "[1]This is how one should regard us, as servants of Christ and stewards of the mysteries of God. [2]Moreover it is required of stewards that they be found trustworthy." Paul regards himself and his coworkers as 'servants of Christ' and 'stewards of the mysteries of God.' The stewards of God's mysteries (God's saving plan that is hidden for generations) are required to be faithful.

Paul in Titus 1:7-9 states: "[7]For a bishop, as God's steward, must be blameless; he must not be arrogant or quick-tempered or a drunkard or violent or greedy for gain, [8]but hospitable, a lover of goodness, master of himself, upright, holy, and self-controlled; [9]he must hold firm to the sure word as taught, so that he may be able to give instruction in sound doctrine and also to confute those who contradict it." Paul explains the qualifications for a bishop in the church. He calls a bishop God's steward (οἰκονόμος Θεοῦ). Not only a bishop but also every Christian should have the qualifications of bishop in the church as he/she is the manager/steward in the household of God.

Peter in 1 Peter 4:10-11 states: "[10]As each has received a gift, employ it for one another, as good stewards of God's varied grace: [11]whoever speaks, as one who utters oracles of God; whoever renders service, as one who renders it by the strength which God supplies; in order that in everything God may be glorified through Jesus Christ. To him belong glory and dominion for ever and ever. Amen." A gift of God is given to Christians. Then, Christians should manage the God-given gifts or talents well so that God may be praised through Jesus Christ.

## Chapter Thirteen

# Entrepreneurship and the Use of Resources

### Qualifications of an Entrepreneur

Entrepreneurship is defined as "the creative ability of individuals to seek profits by taking risks and combining resources to produce innovative products."[39] Resources are the basic categories of inputs organized by entrepreneurship to produce goods and services. It may also be defined as "the art of turning an idea into a business" or as "the process by which individuals pursue opportunities without regard to resources they currently control."[40] According to Barringer and Ireland, the characteristics of successful entrepreneurs include passion for the business, product/customer focus, tenacity despite failure, and execution intelligence.[41] Entrepreneurs are passionate in their business, have a creative mind and leadership, persevere although they may fail, and have confidence in what they are doing.

Jeff Rose suggests 10 Bible verses for entrepreneurs:[42]

> 1. "Lazy hands make for poverty, but diligent hands bring wealth." (Proverbs 10:4, NIV)
>
> 2. "Do not toil to acquire wealth; be discerning enough to desist." (Proverbs 23:4, ESV)
>
> 3. "Sluggards do not plow in season; so at harvest time they look but find nothing." (Proverbs 20:4)

---

39 Irvin B. Tucker, *Economics for Today* (10th ed.). Cengage Learning, 2019, 4.
40 B. R. Barringer and R. D. Ireland, *Entrepreneurship* (3rd ed.). Pearson, 2010, 6.
41 Ibid., 9-13.
42 Jeff Rose, "10 Bible Verses Every Entrepreneur Needs to Read," *Good Financial Cents*. (August 12, 2013). Retrieved from https://www.goodfinancialcents.com/bible-verses-about-business-entrepreneurship.

4. "Whatever you do, work heartily, as for the Lord and not for men, knowing that from the Lord you will receive the inheritance as your reward. You are serving the Lord Christ." (Colossians 3:23-24, ESV)

5. "In vain you rise early and stay up late, toiling for food to eat – for he(=God) grants sleep to those he loves." (Psalm 127:2, NIV)

6. "So whatever you wish that others would do to you, do also to them, for this is the Law and the Prophets." (Matthew 7:12, ESV)

7. "The beginning of wisdom is this: Get wisdom, and whatever you get, get insight." (Proverbs 4:7, ESV)

8. "In all toil there is profit, but mere talk tends only to poverty." (Proverbs 14:23, ESV)

9. "For what does it profit a man to gain the whole world and forfeit his soul?" (Mark 8:36, ESV)

10. "The plans of the diligent lead surely to abundance, but everyone who is hasty comes on to poverty." (Proverbs 21:5, ESV)

Entrepreneurs should be diligent; be wise or discerning; have a willingness to work; work heartily for God not for men; trust God who grants (good) sleep; get wisdom and insight; act instead of mere talk; work not for this world but for the kingdom of God. The plans of the diligent entrepreneurs will lead to abundance.

**Entrepreneurs in the Bible**

Entrepreneurs in the Bible are those who were successful in their businesses (for God) which were monetary or nonmonetary, making a good use of their time, money, wisdom and knowledge, and faith in God. Who are they? Abraham, Isaac, Jacob, Joseph, David, Solomon (while he was young), Jesus Christ, the faithful servants in Jesus' parables of talents and minas, Paul, etc.

### 1. Abraham

The first person in the Bible who became wealthy was probably Abraham. The Bible does not describe in detail how Abraham became rich, but it is easy to guess. First of all, God promised him three things – land, nations, and blessings. The primary strength of Abraham is faith. Abraham was willing to take a risk, having faith in God. When Abraham was called by God, by faith he obeyed God without knowing where he would be going (Genesis 12:1-4; Hebrews 11:8). When Abraham was tested and told to offer his beloved son Isaac as a burnt offering, by faith he obeyed God without knowing what the outcome of his obedience would be (Genesis 22; Hebrews 11:17-19). Abraham became the father of faith (Genesis 15:6). Paul's two pillars of Christianity are Genesis 15:6 and Habakkuk 2:4 in Romans (1:17; 4:3, 5, 9, 22) and Galatians (3:6, 11).

Genesis 13:2 states: "Now Abram was very rich in cattle, in silver, and in gold." Abraham did not waste his possessions but increased them by trusting the LORD. Abraham called on the name of the LORD at Bethel (Genesis 13:4). He was not nearsighted (myopic) but generous. When Abraham's and Lot's flocks and herds increase, there were quarrels between Abraham's herders and Lot's herders. Then, Abraham suggested Lot in Genesis 13:8-9: "[8]Let there be no strife between you and me, and between your herdsmen and my herdsmen; for we are kinsmen. [9]Is not the whole land before you? Separate yourself from me. If you take the left hand, then I will go to the right; or if you take the right hand, then I will go to the left." Abraham allowed Lot, his nephew, to choose land first before him. So, Lot chose the whole plain of the Jordan toward Zoar that was well watered, like the garden of the LORD, like the land of Egypt (Genesis 13:10). However, as we know well, the fate of the land (Sodom and Gomorrah) that Lot chose was total destruction by God's judgment.

What was the result of Abraham's generosity? God tells Abraham in Genesis 13:14-17, after Lot departed from him: "[14]Lift up your eyes, and look from the place where you are, northward and southward and eastward and westward; [15]for all the land which you see I will give to you and to your descendants forever. [16]I will make your descendants as the dust of the earth; so that if one can count the dust of the earth, your descendants also can be counted. [17]Arise, walk through the length and the breadth of the land, for I will give it to you." Abraham did not let God's promises go away without being fulfilled. He held God's promises fast and kept them in mind. Abraham stayed near the great trees of Mamre at Hebron, where he built an altar to the LORD (Genesis 13:18) to worship him.

### 2. Isaac

Isaac's life was an imitation of Abraham. His life imitated Abraham's strengths and weaknesses. God's blessing on Isaac was probably due to his father's faith. Like his father Abraham, Isaac was a coward that he lied to Abimelech king of Philistines and his men that his wife Rebekah was his sister as he was worried that the Philistines would otherwise kill him to take Rebekah as she was very beautiful (Genesis 26:1-11). This was a copy of Abraham's lies about his wife Sarah in Genesis 12:10-20 and 20:1-18. Yet, like his father, Isaac had strong faith in God and entrepreneurial spirit. Thus, God blessed Isaac materially. Genesis 26:12-14 states: "[12]Isaac sowed in that land and reaped in the same year a hundredfold. The Lord blessed him, [13]and the man became rich, and gained more and more until he became very wealthy. [14]He had possessions of flocks and herds, and a great household, so that the Philistines envied him." God's blessings on Isaac are very similar to his blessings on Abraham. In that sense, we should live a good and faithful Christian life so that God continuously blesses our children and children's children (Exodus 20:6).

### 3. Jacob

Jacob wanted to obtain Esau's birthright, his twin brother, and thus received Isaac's blessing as the father's blessing was regarded as God's blessing. Jacob persuaded Esau to sell his birthright to him when he was very hungry at the price of red stew (Genesis 25:29-34). As a result, Esau also lost the first-born's blessing to Jacob. Jacob was deceitful and greedy before he knew God. Jacob ran away from Esau when Esau realized that what would be the result of selling his birthright. He lost not only his birthright but also his father's blessing – He found out that he lost everything.

While Jacob was running away from Esau, he was very confused. He probably sought God desperately at this moment of danger. God appeared to Jacob in his dream while he was sleeping at Luz on his way to Haran. God tells Jacob in Genesis 28:13-15: "[13]I am the Lord, the God of Abraham your father and the God of Isaac; the land on which you lie I will give to you and to your descendants; [14]and your descendants shall be like the dust of the earth, and you shall spread abroad to the west and to the east and to the north and to the south; and by you and your descendants shall all the families of the earth bless themselves. [15]Behold, I am with you and will keep you wherever you go and will bring you back to this land; for I will not leave you until I have done that of which I have spoken to you." Next morning Jacob took the stone he placed under his head and set it up as a pillar and poured oil on top of it. He calls the place Bethel (house of God). And he made a vow in Genesis 28:20-22: "[20]If God will be with me, and will keep me in this way that I go, and will give me bread to eat and clothing to wear, [21]so that I come again to my father's house in peace, then the Lord shall be my God, [22]and this stone, which I have set up for a pillar, shall be God's house; and of all that thou givest me I will give the tenth to thee." His faith in God was yet conditional.

Jacob worked diligently and wisely in his uncle Laban's house for 20 years, getting his two daughters (Leah and Rachel) as wives and their two maid servants (Zilpah and Bilhah) from whom he got 11 sons before Jacob and his family departed Laban's house. Jacob was patient at Laban's house, waiting for his return to home. Jacob accumulated large wealth (Genesis 32:1-12). On his way back to home, Jacob was still afraid of facing Esau, knowing his anger. Jacob let all the people cross the ford of the Jabbok. He was left alone, and a man (God's angel) wrestled with him until daybreak (Genesis 32:25). Jacob was adherent. Jacob was holding him fast, saying in Genesis 32:26, "I will not let you go, unless you bless me." So, Jacob gained a new blessed name, "Israel" (יִשְׂרָאֵל), which means "wrestle with God" (Genesis 32:28).

### 4. Joseph

Joseph had dreams (Genesis 37:5-11). His brothers called him "a dreamer" (Genesis 37:19). However, Joseph did not regard his dreams lightly. His dreams to him seemed to be his visions. His brothers tried to test him and his dreams by killing him: "Then we'll see what comes of his dreams" (Genesis 37:20, NIV). And they decided to kill him. But then, they sold Joseph to the Midianite merchants (the Ishmaelites) for twenty shekels of silver (Genesis 37:28, the type of Judas Iscariot's selling Jesus for the thirty pieces of silver, Matthew 27:3). Joseph never gave up his dreams or visions even in the midst of sufferings and imprisonment.

Joseph finally became the prime minister of Egypt, when he interpreted Pharaoh's dreams and made them prepare for the seven-year famine (Genesis 40-41). Proverbs 29:18 states: "Where there is no vision (or dream), the people perish; but he that keepeth the law, happy is he" (KJV).

5. **David**

David was a man of prayers. He always believed God's being with him and his protection even at the moment when he was walking through the valley of the shadow of death (Psalm 23:4). As a boy, he could defeat Goliath with a sling and with a stone (1 Samuel 17:50). David's victory over Goliath was due to his strong faith in God (1 Samuel 17:45-47). David was very successful as a king although he committed the critical trespasses of adultery (Bathsheba) and murder of an innocent one (Uriah, Bathsheba's husband) (2 Samuel 11). It was because David was immediate in repentance and always wanted to pray to God, realizing his sins and trespasses, and be restored in his relationship with God.

Yet David failed again when he became old and wanted to number his soldiers (2 Samuel 24; 1 Chronicles 21). When David ordered Joab to number the people, Joab's report was that there were eight hundred thousand valiant men in Israel (among ten tribes) and five hundred thousand in Judah (among the tribes of Judah and Benjamin) (2 Samuel 24:9). So, David's army was one million and three hundred thousand strong men. However, God did not like this numbering at all. Why? When we trust God and lean on him, we can be successful even in the midst of difficult situations. However, if we depend upon our human ability and strengths, we will fail in our entrepreneurial life.

In spite of David's numerous sins and trespasses, God still loved David more than anybody else. God always wanted to take an example of David when he commands other people. God in 1 Kings 3:14 tells Solomon, "And if you will walk in my ways, keeping my statutes and my commandments, as your father David walked, then I will lengthen your days." God in 1 Kings 11:38 tells Jeroboam, the first king of the northern kingdom, Israel: "And if you will hearken to all that I command you, and will walk in my ways, and do what is right in my eyes by keeping my statutes and my commandments, as David my servant did, I will be with you, and will build you a sure house, as I built for David, and I will give Israel to you." Again, David was a man of prayers and he did not hesitate in repenting before God when he realized his sins and trespasses.

### 6. Solomon

What were Solomon's strengths that differentiated him from others? God appeared to Solomon in his dream, telling him to ask for whatever he wants God to give him (1 Kings 3:5). Then, Solomon asked God to give him "a discerning heart (or wisdom) to govern God's people and to distinguish between right and wrong" (1 Kings 3:9). Then, God was very much pleased with Solomon. God in 1 Kings 3:12 tells Solomon: "[12]I will give you a wise and discerning heart, so that there will never have been anyone like you, nor will there ever be. [13]Moreover, I will give you what you have not asked for – both wealth and honor – so that in your lifetime you will have no equal among kings." Solomon's wisdom and wise judgment was praised by many people and his reputation was widely known even to other countries. His country and people were very prospering (1 Kings 4-10).

However, Solomon's mind departed God as he began to worship idols that were brought in with his marriages with foreign women – Solomon had three hundred wives and seven hundred concubines (1 Kings 11:3). When Solomon's mind left God, God's blessings also departed from Solomon. Solomon's kingdom was divided into two. Only two tribes (Judah and Benjamin) were given to Solomon's son Rehoboam (the Kingdom of Judah, the southern kingdom) and the other ten tribes were given to Jeroboam (the Kingdom of Israel, the northern kingdom). Human wealth and glory are temporary. Even

Solomon who was commended by God when he was asking for a discerning heart failed when he turned away from God. Our success as a Christian entrepreneur is guaranteed as long as we reside in God (John 15:6-7).

### 7. A Woman in Proverbs 31

Proverbs 31:1-31 describes a woman of noble character. She is a trustful wife who brings good to her husband all the days of her life (vv. 11-12). She is a very diligent, energetic, and hard worker (vv. 13-17). She knows how to make her trading profitable (v. 18). She takes care of the poor and needy people (v. 20) and her household, as well (v. 21). She fears God and is praised by other people including her husband (vv. 28-31). Proverbs 31 probably describes an ideal wife of noble character, but she is a great fit for an entrepreneur if there such person exists.

### 8. Jesus

What was Jesus' goal as an entrepreneur? What was the purpose of his short life and three plus years of his public ministry? Jesus provokingly taught and spread the kingdom of God. Even after he was risen, Jesus continued to teach about the kingdom of God for forty more days before he was taken up into heaven (Acts 1:1-11). Jesus' disciples did not seem to understand his teaching about the Kingdom of God. But Jesus never gave up his teaching. His ministry seemed to end when he was crucified. However, as we all know well, his ministry and teaching of the kingdom of God continued through his disciples and disciples' disciples until today.

### 9. Servants in Jesus' Parable

The servants in Jesus' parable of talents in Matthew 25:14-30 (also, in Luke 19:11-27) were also entrepreneurs who worked hard, running business to make profits. The Bible did not tell what kind of business they were doing, but the first servant who received five talents was successful in gaining profit – five more talents (around five million dollars' profit) starting with the fund of five million dollars. The second servant who received two talents was also successful in gaining profit – two more talents (around two million dollars' profit) starting with the fund of two million dollars. The master did not direct them what kind of business they should do. Those two servants who gained profits probably did not do the same business. However, as they worked hard as a good and faithful entrepreneur, each of them could gain profit (Matthew 25:21 & 23).

### 10. Paul

Who was Paul? He was an arrogant Pharisee who thought Jesus blasphemed God while he was alive and now his disciples were blaspheming God by claiming that Jesus is the Son of God. He was trying to persecute his disciples. However, when he met Jesus who appeared to him in the form of light on his way to Damascus to persecute more Christians, his life turned upside down. His life changed from the one who persecuted to the one who was persecuted.

Paul's life seemed to be a series of failures. His spreading the gospel among Jews was rejected and the churches that he had founded still had a lot of problems other than the churches in Macedonia. Paul spent more than half of his Christian life in prisons in Jerusalem, Rome, Asia Minor, etc. Many believers probably complained about their life to God and gave up their work for God if they were in Paul's situation. But Paul never gave up in prisons. Rather, he encouraged and comforted other Christians who were about to let their Christian beliefs go. Paul spent more than half of his Christian life in prisons in Jerusalem, Rome, Asia Minor, etc. Many believers probably complained about their life to God and gave up their work for God if they were in Paul's situation. Paul in 2 Timothy 4:2 tells us: "Preach the word, be urgent in season and out of season, convince, rebuke, and exhort, be unfailing in patience and in teaching." Paul had written about half of the books (13 books) in the New Testament in the form of letters which were circulated among people in the house churches in towns. How could it be possible? His spirit of persistent and adventurous entrepreneurship made this possible.

# Chapter Fourteen

# Efficiency versus Equity

## Efficiency and Equity in Economics

Efficiency in economics is concerned with the optimal production and distribution of resources. Productive or economic efficiency occurs when the largest amount of goods and services are produced with a given amount of inputs or resources. Allocative efficiency occurs when goods and services are distributed according to consumer preferences. Allocative efficiency can be obtained when no one can be made better off without making someone else worse off, which is also known as Pareto efficiency. Productive and allocative efficiency can be attainable when we assume perfect competition. Equity occurs if a society distributes its economic resources or benefits fairly among its people. Equity and fairness are often interchangeably used.

Efficiency and equity do not seem to go hand in hand. How can the market economy with perfect competition attain equity in a society (although it can attain both productive and allocative efficiency)? To attain equity in the society, those people who make more money are willing to pay higher taxes and the taxes may be used to help the poor for the society as a whole to be better off. However, as Shane Hall states, higher tax rates on high income people will reduce their incentive or reward for working hard and thus result in less production.[43] Torben Anderson and Jonas Maibom explain that when countries are inside the opportunity set, that is, when the country is both less efficient (in terms of economic performance) and less equitable (in terms of income equality), then there is a scope of improvements in both economic performance (efficiency) and income

[43] Shane Hall, "Economics: Equity vs. Efficiency," *Bizfluent.* (September 26, 2017). Retrieved from https://bizfluent.com/about-7230309-economics--equity-vs--efficiency.html.

equality (equity).[44] Otherwise, more equal (or fair) distribution of income can be possible at the cost of economic performance (efficiency).

John Buck states: "People who think markets provide a generally fair distribution of output among the population tend to oppose government intervention in the marketplace. This is the position of most traditional conservatives, who usually favor a very limited government role in the economy. People who think markets create an unfair distribution of output tend to favor a larger role for government in the redistribution of wealth. Traditional liberals tend to favor this position."[45] That is, the conservative Republicans prefer the small government claiming markets already provide fairness whereas the liberal Democrats prefer the big government claiming markets cannot resolve the issue of unfairness. Many economists believe competitive markets are efficient, however they may not be fair in distribution.

## Efficiency and Equity in the Bible

### 1. Efficiency

Jethro, Moses' father-in-law, in Exodus 18:13-27 advised Moses to select capable and honest men to help him when he judged the Israelites to be more effective and save time. That is, by sharing heavy burden with others according their ability, we can do the work for God more efficiently. Jethro in Exodus 18:21-22 tells Moses: "[21]Moreover choose able men from all the people, such as fear God, men who are trustworthy and who hate a bribe; and place such men over the people as rulers of thousands, of hundreds, of fifties, and of tens. [22]And let them judge the people at all times; every great matter they shall bring to you, but any small matter they shall decide themselves; so it will be easier for you, and they will bear the burden with you."

---

[44] Torben M. Anderson and Jonas Maibom, "The Trade-Off between Efficiency and Equity," *VOX*. (May 29, 2016). Retrieved from https://voxeu.org/article/trade-between-efficiency-and-equity.

[45] John Buck, "Economic Efficiency and Equity," *Economic Perspectives*. (February 10, 2008). Retrieved from http://econperspectives.blogspot.com/2008/02/economic-efficiency-and-equity.html.

The twelve apostles in Acts 6:1 were busy with both the daily distribution of food and preaching, so they could do neither duty well. Yet, there were complaints by the Hellenistic Jews against the Hebraic Jews. So, they decided to choose seven men among the disciples who were known to be full of the Spirit and wisdom and let them do the responsibility of the daily distribution of food (Acts 6:3). Then, the 12 apostles could give their attention to prayer and the ministry of word (Acts 6:4). This is a way of doing God's work – prayer, the ministry of word, and distribution of food – more efficiently not being burdened too much by a routine work.

Paul in 1 Corinthians 12:4-31 and Ephesians 4:1-16 mentions various spiritual gifts given to the members of the church, and unity and diversity of the body of Christ. God allowed various gifts to various members of the church, the body of Christ, for them to work for God efficiently when they understand the will of God and each of them does his/her best with God-given gifts. Paul could accomplish many things in his ministry for God as he cooperated with his coworkers (Paul with Barnabas in Acts 13-15; Paul with Silas, and Timothy later in Acts 16-17; Paul with Aquila and Priscilla in Acts 18; Paul with Luke and other coworkers in Acts 20-28).

## 2. Equity

Equity is one of the important biblical themes, and thus we can find many examples. 2 Samuel 8:15 (also 1 Chronicles 18:14) states: "David reigned over all of Israel, administering justice and equity (צְדָקָה, tsedaqah) to every one of his people" (ISV). The Hebrew word צְדָקָה (tsedaqah) is also translated as 'righteousness,' 'honesty,' or 'justice.'[46] That is, an equitable activity may be regarded as righteous, honest, or just.

The Psalmist in Psalm 9:8 states: "He (=God) rules the world in righteousness (צֶדֶק, tsedeq) and judges his people with equity (מֵישָׁר, meshar). The Hebrew word מֵישָׁר (meshar) is also translated as

[46] Strong's Hebrew Concordance, "6666. tsedaqah," *BibleHub*. Retrieved from https://biblehub.com/hebrew/6666.htm

'uprightness,' 'fairness,' 'equity,' or 'evenness.'[47] The meanings of the two Hebrew words are similar to each other. By using the two similar words together, God's fair or impartial (and his people's) government is emphasized. Prophet Isaiah in Isaiah 11:1-5 prophesies about the coming Messiah (Christ), and states: "but with righteousness he will judge the needy and decide with equity for earth's poor." (11:4a, ISV)

As we discussed in Chapter 10, God is fair or equitable in distribution. Exodus 16:18 states: "And when they measured it by the omer, the one who gathered much did not have too much, and the one who gathered little did not have too little. Everyone had gathered just as much as they needed." Furthermore, God wants his people to share their possessions with the poorer ones. This is a way in which God's equity can be realized. Moses in Deuteronomy 15:7-8 states: "[7]If there is among you a poor man, one of your brethren, in any of your towns within your land which the LORD your God gives you, you shall not harden your heart or shut your hand against your poor brother, [8]but you shall open your hand to him, and lend him sufficient for his need, whatever it may be."

Thus, Paul emphasizes his economics of equality, sharing what you are rich now with those who are poor in what you are rich so that they may share what they will abound with you who may be poor in what they will abound in the future. Paul's teaching of equality is to reduce inequality whether it is material wealth or spiritual wealth.

### 3. Efficiency versus Equity

As we reviewed at the beginning of this chapter, there is usually a trade-off between efficiency and equity. That is, to increase efficiency, equity may be reduced; or to increase equity (or to reduce inequality), efficiency may be reduced as people may lose their incentives to work hard and thus become less productive. We see this in the example of socialism or communism where people's incentives to work hard may be reduced as they cannot possess their own wealth.

---

[47] Ibid., "4339. meshar," *BibleHub*. Retrieved from https://biblehub.com/hebrew/4339.htm

However, as we see in Acts 2:43-47 and 4:32-35, efficiency and equity can be in harmony when people's incentives to work hard are not denied but encouraged further by their noble goal or purpose of life. When Christians initiate their love of neighbors by voluntarily sharing their possessions with them, they may work harder to make more profit and share more plenty with more people.

## Chapter Fifteen

# Markets in the Bible

### Markets in Economics

A market in economics is a place where buyers and sellers gather together to trade goods and services or factors including labor. A product market is a market for goods or services whereas a factor market is a market for the factors of production such as labor, capital, natural resources, and entrepreneurial ability. As we reviewed in Chapter 9, the Bible does not reject the private ownership, unlike socialism and communism, and the market economy in which price and quantity are determined in the market not by the central authority. Jesus tells the parables of servants (Matthew 25; Luke 19) who were entrusted their master's money to do business. They probably started their businesses in the market.

### Markets in the Old Testament

The Hebrew word מַעֲרָב (maarab) means merchandise or market (Ezekiel 27:9, 13, 17, 19, 25, 27, 33, 34). The King James Version (KJV) translates the word in Ezekiel 27:13, 17, 19, and 25 as 'market' and the other verses as 'merchandise'; on the other hand, The New International Version (NIV) translates it as 'wares.'[48]

From the Hebrew word סָחַר (sachar, Strong number 5503), it also means an emporium, abstractly profit (from trade), trade, mart, or merchandise (Genesis 23:16, 34:10 & 21, 37:28, 42:34; 1 Kins10:28; 2 Chronicles 1:16, 9:14; Psalm 38:10; Proverbs 31:14; Isaiah 23:2 & 8, 47:15; Jeremiah 14:18; Ezekiel 27:12, 16, 18, 21(twice), 36, 38:13).[49] The Hebrew word סחר (sachar, Strong number 5504) means 'gain,'

---

[48] Ibid., "4627. maarab," *BibleHub.* Retrieved from https://biblehub.com/hebrew/4627.htm

[49] Ibid., "5503. sachar," *BibleHub.* Retrieved from https://biblehub.com/hebrew/5503.htm

'market,' 'merchandise,' or 'profit' (Proverbs 3:14, 31:18; Isaiah 23:18 (twice)).[50] The Hebrew word סָחַר (sachar, Strong number 5505) again means 'merchandise' or 'mart' (Proverbs 3:14; Isaiah 23:3 and 45:14).[51]

A market, market place, trade, and profit have no negative connotations in the Old Testament. People made profit by trading in a market. God blessed or cursed them depending upon how they made profit and how they used the money that they earned.

## Markets in the New Testament

The Jewish merchants made the temple yard a market or marketplace where they sold oxen, sheep, and doves/pigeons to those who came to the temple to offer and worship (John 2:14-16). Jesus in John 2:16 tells the merchants: "Get these out of here! Stop turning my Father's house into a market!" Jesus rebukes them when they did not distinguish the temple and the market when those two have different purposes and uses.

In the market at Corinth and other Gentile cities meat that was offered to idols was sold along with meat that was not offered to idols (1 Corinthians 8 & 10:25-26; Romans 14). People with little faith were in trouble without knowing whether or not they should buy meat in the market as they did not know which meat was offered to idols and which not. Paul in 1 Corinthians 10:25-26 advised them; "[25]Eat whatever is sold in the meat market without raising any question on the ground of conscience. [26]For 'the earth is the Lord's, and everything in it.'" As everything belongs to God and there is no other god, God's people can eat whatever he allows them. The same Paul also advises us in Romans 14:20-21: "[20]Do not destroy, for the sake of food, destroy the work of God. Everything is indeed clean, but it is wrong for anyone to make others fall by what he eats; [21]it is right not to eat meat or drink wine or do anything that makes your brother stumble." Although we can eat whatever that is allowed by God, if weak brothers

---

[50] Ibid., "5504. sachar," *BibleHub.* Retrieved from https://biblehub.com/hebrew/5504.htm

[51] Ibid., "5505. sachar," *BibleHub.* Retrieved from https://biblehub.com/hebrew/5505.htm

or sisters are stumbled by what we eat or drink, it is better for us not to eat or drink for them.

Agora (αγορά), from its root meaning 'to collect,' is a 'town meeting place,' 'resort of the people,' so a place where the public generally met to exchange views and wares. Market, 'agora' (αγορά) in Greek and 'forum' in Latin, is "a large open area in many ancient cities, especially of Greece and Rome, having the public market on one side only, the other sides of the area being occupied by temples, theatres, colonnades, courts of justice, baths, and other public structures, the whole square often presenting a magnificent appearance."[52] The Greek word ἀγορά (agora) is any collection of men, congregation, or assembly; or place where assemblies are held. The market place in New Testament times was the public open place not only for the exchange of merchandise but also for one or more of the following purposes:

> (1) a place where the children came together to sing, dance and play (Matthew 11:16; Luke 7:32);
>
> (2) a place for loafers, a sort of ancient, irresponsible labor bureau where the out-of-work idler waited the coming of an employer with whom he might bargain for his services, usually by the day (Matthew 20:1-16);
>
> (3) a place where the proud pretender could parade in long robes and get public recognition, "salutations in the market places" (Matthew 23:3-7; Mark 12:38; Luke 11:43, 20:46);
>
> (4) a place where the sick were brought for treatment, the poor man's sanatorium, a municipal hospital (Mark 6:56);
>
> (5) a place of preliminary hearing in trials, where the accused might be brought before rulers who were present at the time (Acts 16:19);

---

[52] ATS Bible Dictionary, "Market," *BibleHub*. Retrieved from https://biblehub.com/topical/m/market.htm.

(6) a place for religious and probably political or philosophical discussion, a forum, a free-speech throne (Acts 17:17).[53]

Jesus in Matthew 11:16-17 (also in Luke 7:32-33) says: "16To what can I compare this generation? They are like children sitting in the marketplaces and calling out to others: 17'We played the pipe for you, and you did not dance; we sang a dirge, and you did not mourn.'" A market was a place where many people including children gathered for various purposes.

Jesus in Matthew 20:1-16 tells a parable of the kingdom of Heaven. The market in this story is a place where jobless workers waited to be picked by someone who would need labor for his place or project – it was a labor market where unemployed looked for temporary jobs. Average workers were paid one denarius per day. In this story, the landowner went out to the marketplace to hire some workers around 9 AM in the morning. He went out to the marketplace to hire more workers about noon, about 3 PM, and then 5 PM. The story does not tell why the vineyard owner hired more workers at 5 PM although the day's work would end soon about 6 PM before it became dark. He was probably very generous and merciful like our God. The marketplace here seems to be the world where we live our daily life. The vineyard owner is God who is willing to give us an opportunity to work for him until the last moment. God tries to call more workers for him. Even though someone accepts him at the last moment, he will treat him/her fairly although God's fairness does not seem to be fair to some people. Jesus ends the story, saying: "So, the last will be first, and the first last." (Matthew 20:16). Knowing that this story is to explain the Kingdom of God, the time when we accept Jesus Christ does not really matter, but what matters is how faithfully and diligently we labor for God's Kingdom and gospel.

A market was a place where people wanted to show off themselves and get people's recognition like in today's society or community. Jesus in Matthew 23:5-7 says: "5They do all their deeds to be seen by men; for they make their phylacteries broad and their fringes long, 6and they love the place of honor at feasts and the best seats in the synagogues,

[53] Ibid.

[7]and salutations in the market places, and being called rabbi by men." A market is our community or society where we get along with other people. What we do and how we speak are seen and heard by other people, and thus we are evaluated by them. Our Christian conduct in the marketplace – that is, in the community or the society – may bring more people to Jesus Christ or turn away from Jesus Christ.

A market was a place where sick people were brought to have a chance to be healed or poor people came to get a relief our community or society where we get along with other people. Jesus met the needy people and sick people in marketplaces, where he healed the sick people and comforted the people who were in need. Mark 6:56 states: "And wherever he (=Jesus) came, in villages, cities, or country, they laid the sick in the market places, and besought him that they might touch even the fringe of his garment; and as many as touched it were made well." The marketplace is where we live today. We may comfort and find a way to help people who are in needy situations.

A market was a place of preliminary hearing in trials, where the accused might be brought before rulers who were present at the time. Acts 16:19 describes: "But when her (the female fortune-teller's) owners saw that their hope of gain was gone, they seized Paul and Silas and dragged them into the market place before the rulers."

A market was a place for religious, philosophical, or political debates, a forum, a free-speech throne. Paul in Athens used this place to teach about Jesus Christ who was not known to the people there yet. Acts 17:17 states: "So he (=Paul) argued in the synagogue with the Jews and the devout persons, and in the market place every day with those who chanced to be there." A market is a place where we meet people whom we know or do not know. It may be our neighborhood, school, workplace, or community. We may have an opportunity to witness Jesus Christ there. Paul in 2 Timothy 4:2 advises us: "Preach the word, be urgent in season and out of season, convince, rebuke, and exhort, be unfailing in patience and in teaching."

Above all, a market is a place where we buy and sell goods and services. As a buyer or consumer our goal is to maximize our utility – satisfaction or happiness – within the given budget constraint. To do so, our consumption pattern should be diligent and modest. As a seller or a business owner our goal is to maximize profit. Trying to gain more profit is not unethical as long as we do business honestly and fairly as well as do work for God faithfully. Proverbs 11:1 states: "A false balance is an abomination to the Lord, but a just weight is his delight"; and again, Proverbs 20:23 says: "Diverse weights are an abomination to the Lord, and false scales are not good." Jesus in his parables of talents (Matthew 25:14-30) and minas (Luke 19:11-27) encourages to make more profit. Although the stories are parables and Jesus meant that the servants' hard work was for God, doing business in the market and gaining profit will be equally important not only for our household but also for the household of God as God wants us to be prosperous in this world. Jesus in Luke 16:10 tells his disciples and us: "He who is faithful in a very little is faithful also in much; and he who is dishonest in a very little is dishonest also in much." When we – as buyers and/or sellers – do our best in the marketplace (in a very little) faithfully and honestly, we can do our best in the ministry of God (in much) faithfully and honestly.

Chapter Sixteen

# Economics of Uncertainty and Game Theory

## Decision Making Under Uncertainty

As I previously mentioned, economics is about decision making in our daily living. Our decision making may not always be done under certainty but sometimes under uncertainty or risk. More precisely speaking, risk is measurable (uncertainty) whereas (genuine) uncertainty is unmeasurable. As a matter of fact, our life may be more uncertain or risky rather than certain or safe. We are not able to foresee what will happen tomorrow. Nobody knows what will wait for us when we die. We believe that we will be in paradise (in spirit) or the kingdom of God (in spiritual body) as Jesus promises us (Luke 23:43; John 3:16, 5:24, 14:2-3).

## Uncertainty in the Bible

Did Adam know what would happen to him when he eats (the fruit) of the tree of the knowledge of good and evil although God told him that he would surely die when he eats of it (Genesis 1:17)? Absolutely not! If he had known what would wait for him, he would have forbidden Eve from eating of it and he himself would not have eaten of it, or he had forsaken Eve not to be tempted by the serpent along with her.

Did Noah know for sure there would be the great flood? Probably not. He built an ark for one hundred years without knowing when there would be the great flood. The Book of Hebrews describes about Noah's faith in Hebrews 11:7: "By faith Noah, being warned by God concerning events as yet unseen, took heed and constructed an ark for the saving of his household; by this he condemned the world and became an heir of the righteousness which comes by faith." Noah patiently built the ark for a century and thus could save himself and his family.

God promised to Abraham three things – land, nations, and blessings. Did Abraham know whether God surely would give him and/or his descendants all those three promises? Probably not. Although Abraham was a man of faith, he was not quite sure whether God would keep his promise. That was why he was a little upset when God appeared to him in Genesis 15:1 and asked him in Genesis 15:2 about his promise of offspring/nations: "O Lord GOD, what wilt thou give me, for I continue childless, and the heir of my house is Elie'zer of Damascus?" Then, he said sarcastically in Genesis 15:3: "Behold, thou hast given me no offspring; and a slave born in my house will be my heir." The greatness of Abraham is not that he knew God more than other people or his conduct was perfect but that he believed God with a simple mind whenever God promised although he did not know what would happen to him on the next day. God credited Abraham's faith to him as righteousness (Genesis 15:6). The Book of Hebrews describes about Abraham's faith in Hebrews 11:8-19: "[8]By faith Abraham obeyed when he was called to go out to a place which he was to receive as an inheritance; and he went out, not knowing where he was to go. … [17]By faith Abraham, when he was tested, offered up Isaac, and he who had received the promises was ready to offer up his only son." Abraham's decision making of departing his home land, Ur of the Chaldeans, offering of his son Isaac, and others was done under uncertainty, without knowing what the outcomes would be.

Many people of God – Isaac, Jacob, Joseph, Moses, Joshua, Caleb, Rahab, Samuel, David, and others – kept their faith and obeyed God, believing God's promises without knowing what would happen to them in the future. Today, many Christians live by faith under uncertainty, believing that they would enter the kingdom of God.

## Game Theory

Game theory in economics tries to explain an individual's or a firm's behavior or decision making when they do not know the other party's behavior or decision making. The prisoner's dilemma is a basic standard game in which two rational players/persons make decisions for their own self-interests when they are placed in two separate rooms without being allowed to communicate with each other. That is, two individuals or players make a rational decision under uncertainty about the other player's decision, seeing the possible outcomes depending upon their decisions. This kind of game is called a noncooperative game.

I was interested in interpreting believers' decision making under uncertainty in the Bible using game theory when I was a graduate student who studied game theory. While I was preparing for this book, I found that there were few scholars who discussed about game theory in the Bible.[54] However, I want to explain game theory for the following examples using my own payoff tables.

### 1. Adam versus God

To form a payoff table for the game between Adam and God, my *a-priori* (prepositional) assumptions are that God exists and God's promise or command may be either fulfilled or not fulfilled (bluffed).

| | | **God** | |
|---|---|---|---|
| | | **Fulfill** | **Not Fulfill** |
| **Adam** | **Obey** | **$(+\infty, +\infty)$** | **$(-\alpha_1, +\theta_1)$** |
| | **Disobey** | **$(-\infty, -\infty)$** | **$(+\alpha_2, -\theta_2)$** |

[54] Bob Becking, "Biblical Games: Game Theory and the Hebrew Bible," *Ars Disputandi*, Vol. 3 (2003), 91-93. In his article, Becking discusses about Steven J. Brams' book, *Biblical Games: Game Theory and the Hebrew Bible* (Cambridge MA 1982).

God's command to Adam is in Genesis 2:16b-17, "[16b]You may freely eat of every tree of the garden; [17]but <u>of the tree of the knowledge of good and evil you shall not eat</u>, for in the day that you eat of it <u>you shall die</u>."

When Adam obeys God and God's command is valid, Adam will enjoy eternal life in the garden of Eden. So, his payoff is infinity ($+\infty$) or extremely large. As God is very much well pleased with Adam's obedience, his payoff is also infinity ($+\infty$) or extremely large.

When Adam obeys God and God's command is not valid, that is, he will not punish Adam but there is no eternal life for Adam, either. Then, Adam will be very much disappointed and his payoff, $-\alpha_1$, may vary from any negative number to negative infinity, depending upon Adam's character. God is pleased with Adam's obedience although he does not have any intention to fulfill his command or promise. So, his payoff, $+\theta_1$, is some positive number.

> When Adam disobeys God and God's command is valid, Adam will surely die and cannot enjoy eternal life in the garden of Eden. So, his payoff is large negative number or (close to) negative infinity ($-\infty$). As God is very much displeased with Adam's disobedience, his payoff is also (close to) negative infinity ($-\infty$, see Genesis 6:6-7).
>
> When Adam disobeys God and God's command is not valid, that is, God does not punish Adam and there is no eternal life for Adam, either. Then, Adam gains some knowledge as he eats of the tree of the knowledge of good and evil, and thus his payoff, $\alpha_2$, is some positive number. God is displeased with Adam's disobedience although he does not have any intention to fulfill his command or promise. So, his payoff, $-\theta_2$, is some negative number.

What should be Adam's rational decision without knowing God's intention? He does not have a dominant strategy with the given payoff table, which is the best and rational strategy regardless of God's intention. So, his decision is up to his faith in God. In Genesis 3:6, he decided to disobey God's command, eating of the tree of the knowledge of good and evil, and as a result of his disobedience, he was expelled from the garden of Eden (with his wife Eve) and lost eternal life.

### 2. Abraham versus God

For the game between Abraham and God, my *a-priori* (prepositional) assumptions are the same. That is, God exists, and God's promise may be either fulfilled or not fulfilled (bluffed).

| | | **God** | |
|---|---|---|---|
| | | **Fulfill** | **Not Fulfill** |
| **Abraham** | **Faith** | **$(+\infty, +\infty)$** | **$(-\alpha_1, +\theta_1)$** |
| | **No Faith** | **$(-\infty, -\infty)$** | **$(+\alpha_2, -\theta_2)$** |

God's promise to Abraham is in Genesis 12:1-3, "[1]Go from your country and your kindred and your father's house to <u>the land</u> that I will show you. [2]And I will make of you <u>a great nation</u>, and I will <u>bless you</u>, and make your name great, so that <u>you will be a blessing</u>. [3]I will bless those who bless you, and him who curses you I will curse; and by you all the families of the earth shall bless themselves."

When Abraham obeys God and God's promise is valid, Abraham and his descendants will obtain the land of Canaan, become great nations, and enjoy God's blessings. So, his payoff is large positive number or (close to) infinity $(+\infty)$. As God is very much well pleased with Abraham's obedience, his payoff is also (close to) infinity $(+\infty)$.

When Abraham obeys God and God's promise is not valid, that is, he will not keep his promises to Abraham. Then, Abraham will be very much disappointed and his payoff, $-\alpha_1$, may vary from any negative number to negative infinity, depending upon Abraham's character. God is pleased with Abraham's obedience although he does not have any intention to fulfill his promise. So, his payoff, $+\theta_1$, is some positive number.

When Abraham disobeys God and God's promise is valid, Abraham cannot attain God's promise of the land, great nations, and blessings. So, Abraham will be very much disappointed, and his payoff is large negative number or (close to) negative infinity ($-\infty$). As God is very much displeased with Adam's disobedience, his payoff is also (close to) negative infinity ($-\infty$, see Genesis 6:6-7).

When Adam disobeys God and God's promise is not valid, then Abraham did not lose anything. Abraham did not have to leave his home country, Ur of the Chaldeans. He could enjoy extra time for other things in his home town, and thus his payoff, $\alpha_2$, is some positive number. God is displeased with Abraham's disobedience although he does not have any intention to fulfill his promise. So, his payoff, $-\theta_2$, is some negative number.

What should be Abraham's rational decision without knowing God's intention? He does not have a dominant strategy with the given payoff table, like in the case of Adam. So, his decision is up to his faith in God. However, he decided to believe God's promise (Genesis 12:4, 15:6; Hebrews 11:8-19). As a result of his obedience out of faith, he and his descendants attained the land of Canaan, became great nations, and enjoyed God's abundant blessings.

### 3. Person versus God

For the game between any person and God, we may remove the above *a-priori* assumptions. That is, there was indeed historical Jesus, but people are not sure about the existence of God and of Heaven and Hell. Although God exists, Jesus' promise may be valid (existence of Heaven/Hell) or not valid (non-existence of Heaven/Hell). If God does not exist, then Jesus' claim is invalid, and all believers waste their time and life (see 1 Corinthians 15:16-19). I do not consider this case here.

| | | Jesus Christ/God | |
|---|---|---|---|
| | | **Heaven/Hell** | **No Heaven/Hell** |
| **Person** | **Faith** | $(+\infty, +\infty)$ | $(-\alpha_1, +\theta_1)$ |
| | **No Faith** | $(-\infty, -\infty)$ | $(+\alpha_2, -\theta_2)$ |

God's promise to people through Jesus Christ is in John 3:16 and some other similar verses, "For God so loved the world that he gave his only Son, that whoever believes in him should not perish but have eternal life."

When Person has faith in Jesus Christ and Jesus' (or God's) promise is valid, Person will enter the kingdom of Heaven where Person will have eternal life. So, Person's payoff is positive infinity ($+\infty$). As God is very much well pleased with Person's obedience, his payoff is also (close to) positive infinity ($+\infty$).

When Person has faith in Jesus Christ and Jesus' (or God's) promise is not valid, that is, there is neither Heaven nor Hell. Then, Person will be very much disappointed, and thus Person's payoff, $-\alpha_1$, may vary from any negative number to negative infinity, depending upon Person's character. God is pleased with Person's faith although he does not have any intention to fulfill his promise. So, his payoff, $+\theta_1$, is some positive number.

When Person does not have faith in Jesus Christ and Jesus' (or God's) promise is valid, Person cannot go to Heaven but to Hell. So, Person will be very much disappointed, and thus Person's payoff is (close to) negative infinity ($-\infty$) as Person will suffer there eternally. As God is very much displeased with Person's disbelief, his payoff is also (close to) negative infinity ($-\infty$, see Genesis 6:6-7).

When Person does not have faith in Jesus Christ and Jesus' (or God's) promise is not valid, then Person does not lose anything. Rather, Person enjoys the secular worldly life without any guilty feeling, and thus Person's payoff, $\alpha_2$, is some positive number. God is displeased with Person's disbelief although he does not have any intention to fulfill his promise. So, his payoff, $-\theta_2$, is some negative number.

What should be Person's rational decision without knowing God's intention? He does not have a dominant strategy with the given payoff table, like in the cases of Adam and Abraham. So, Person's decision is up to Person's faith in Jesus Christ. Which one between faith and no-faith is a better choice to reduce danger under uncertainty? When you have faith in Jesus Christ but there is no Heaven/Hell, what is your worst loss? Your loss includes your time that you spend for worship and other church activities, money that you offered to the church. When you do not have faith but there is Heaven/Hell, what is your worst loss? Your loss will be unbearable suffering from eternal dying. Although there is no dominant strategy for any individual in this game, a rational choice seems to be obvious.

## Chapter Seventeen

# Environmental Economics

### What Is Environmental Economics?

Environmental economics is an area of economics that deals with economic decisions on the environment. Environmental economics is becoming important as our society or economy is more seriously impacted by global warming, emissions and pollutions, and other environmental issues. Environmental problems arise when people pursue their own interest or profit without considering other people and environments. Factories pollute rivers or seas with tons of chemicals. People cut too many trees in a forest or catch too many fish in an ocean where the property right is vague, which is called the tragedy of commons. That is, some selfish individuals exploit a shared common resource to the point of exhaustion. Recently people have been paying more attention to environmental issues and social responsibility. We can reduce the environmental issues by caring other people and creatures.

Traditionally, a firm's behavior is to maximize its profit without much thinking about environmental and social responsibility. As global warming is becoming a serious issue, a firm's goal that includes avoiding damages to environment by reducing emissions/negative externalities is very desirable. Firms' attention to people (social responsibility) and planet (environmental consideration) is recent. The triple bottom line (TBL) outcomes are the profits (profit), the avoidance of damage to the environment (planet), and the achievement of social benefits (people). The TBL outcomes will be a good way to do business that is beneficial not only to themselves - companies and their employees - but also to society and other members of society and to environments.

Although the TBL outcomes are ideal and ethical objectives for any firm that exists within a society, it may not be easy to find such firms in the real world - maybe more from not-for-profit firms and less from for-profit firms. Smaller companies may have more difficulties than larger companies in pursuing the TBL outcomes as they try to lower their production costs to be more competitive for survival while the TBL outcomes are costly. However, if they bear with less profit and start to pursue a triple-bottom-line outcome now, they may make more profit later by attracting more customers.

### The Environment in the Garden of Eden

The prosperity of human beings is closely related with the environment as God initially gave the right to Adam and Eve to rule over the environment – all the creatures, including animals, birds, fishes, trees and plants (Genesis 1:28-29). God created the garden of Eden for his first household, Adam and Eve, and the good environment for all creatures such as the fish of the sea, the birds of the air, the animals, trees and plants on the ground. God entrusted the first people to take care of the environment. Not only human beings but also all other creatures were supposed to live eternally without aging or being decayed.

God tells Adam to take care of the environment, including the garden of Eden. Genesis 2:15 states: "The LORD God took the man and put him in the garden of Eden to till it and keep it." The Hebrew word for "keep" is שָׁמַר (shamar) which also means "watch" or "preserve."[55] God wanted to see his people and other environments living healthy, clean, and prospering life according to God's blessings.

### Protection of the Environment in the Bible

God loved his creation – not only human beings but also all other creation. God continued to communicate with his people and lead them even after Adam and Eve fell. God wanted his people to continue to take care of his other creation – environments.

Protection of the environment starts with people. When we respect and love other people, we may not harm or hurt them. Smoking in a public place, littering a can or a bottle on a highway,

[55] Strong's Hebrew Concordance. "8104. shamar," *BibleHub.* Retrieved from https://biblehub.com/hebrew/8104.htm

honking unnecessarily, or making a loud noise during night time may hurt or bother other people. These negative externalities are the activities that people may do when they do not care about others. The Bible tells us to love your neighbors, brothers and sisters, strangers, and even enemies (Leviticus 19:18 & 34; Matthew 5:43-44, 22:39; Mark 12:31; Luke 6:27 & 35, 10:27; John 13:34, 15:12; Romans 12:10, 13:9-10, 15:2; Galatians 5:14; Hebrews 13:1-2; James 2:8; 1 Peter 1:22, 4:8; 1 John 2:10, 3:11, 14 & 23, 4:7, 11 & 21).

God gives complete rest to the land during the seventh year to be environmentally healthier and more productive later. God in Leviticus 25:1-7 instructs the Israelites that the land must have a Sabbath year of complete rest in the seventh year (vv. 2, 4, 5). During its Sabbath year the land still produces on its own without being cultivated, and any crops that grow shall be free for all, including servants, slaves, foreigners, cattle and wild animals. God is caring for all his creation.

God in Numbers 35:33-34 tells his people: "[33]You shall not thus pollute the land in which you live; for blood pollutes the land, and no expiation can be made for the land, for the blood that is shed in it, except by the blood of him who shed it. [34]You shall not defile the land in which you live, in the midst of which I dwell; for I the Lord dwell in the midst of the people of Israel." The land represents all environments. The Hebrew word חָנֵף (chaneph) in Verse 33 means "pollute," "defile."[56] This Hebrew word is also used in Psalm 106:38, Isaiah 24:5, Jeremiah 3:1-2 and 9, and Micah 4:11 in connection with the land. The land or the environment may be polluted by people's behavior such as murder/blood (Psalm 106:38; Numbers 35:33), disobedience of the laws and violation of the statutes and the covenant (Isaiah 24:5), prostitution and wickedness (Jeremiah 3:1-2), adultery (Jeremiah 3:9), and defilement (Micah 4:1).

---

[56] Ibid., "2610. chaneph." *BibleHub*. Retrieved from https://biblehub.com/hebrew/2610.htm

**Punishment of the Environment in the Bible**

God in Genesis 3:17 says to Adam: "Because you have listened to the voice of your wife, and have eaten of the tree of which I commanded you, 'You shall not eat of it,' cursed is the ground because of you" When Adam and Eve fell, the ground was also cursed, and all creation was destined to be decayed, although it was not God's original plan of creation. There was no creature that could live forever. The destiny of the environment was connected with the destiny of human beings.

Isaiah in Isaiah 24:1 states: "Behold, the Lord will lay waste the earth and make it desolate, and he will twist its surface and scatter its inhabitants."; in 24:3-5: "[3]The earth shall be utterly laid waste and utterly despoiled; for the Lord has spoken this word. [4]The earth mourns and withers, the world languishes and withers; the heavens languish together with the earth. [5]The earth lies polluted under its inhabitants; for they have transgressed the laws, violated the statutes, broken the everlasting covenant." Although God wants his people to take a good care of the environment, God punishes the land and other environments not because of their faults but because of human faults as human beings and other environments are destined to have the same end.

Literally interpreting the Bible, the human lifespan has been reduced significantly after the great flood. Most people in Genesis 5 lived more than 800 years – Adam (930), Seth (912), Enosh (905), Kenan (910), Mahalalel (895), Jared (962), Methuselah (969), and Lamech (777). Some biblical scholars do not see these numbers are not their actual lifespans, but 900 plus years age was already a significant reduction comparing to the eternal life that God originally planned for the first human beings in the garden of Eden.

Then, as sin increased on the earth (Genesis 6:5, 11), God decided to limit the human lifespan to 120 years. God in Genesis 6:3 states: "My Spirit will not put up with humans for such a long time, for they are only mortal flesh. In the future, their normal lifespan will be no more than 120 years" (NLT). God grieved (or regretted) that he had made man on the earth (Genesis 6:6). When Noah began to build an ark, he was about 500 years old. He completed it at his age of 600 years old.

Noah lived another 350 years after the great flood and died at the age of 950. However, after Noah the human lifespan gradually decreased toward 120 years maximum. People in Genesis 11 lived 400 plus years, and then 200 plus years. Terah, Abraham's father, lived 205 years (Genesis 11:32). Abraham lived 175 years (Genesis 25:7), Isaac 180 years (Genesis 35:28), Jacob 147 years (Genesis 47:28), Joseph 110 years (Genesis 50:26), Moses 120 years (Deuteronomy 34:7), and Joshua 110 years (Judges 2:8). David lived about 70 years. The Psalmist in Psalm 90:10 says: "The years of our life are threescore and ten, or even by reason of strength fourscore; yet their span is but toil and trouble; they are soon gone, and we fly away." The average human lifespan decreased further down then recently has been increasing but no more than 90 years yet. And we can hardly see people living more than 120 years.

**Restoration of the Environment**

Can the environmental issues be resolved soon? Although ecologists and environmental scientists make effort to improve our environment and/or resolve the environmental problems, they may only be able to slow down the environmental problems not remove them fundamentally. Paul in Romans 8:19-23 states: "[19]For the creation waits with eager longing for the revealing of the sons of God; [20]for the creation was subjected to futility, not of its own will but by the will of him who subjected it in hope; [21]because the creation itself will be set free from its bondage to decay and obtain the glorious liberty of the children of God. [22]We know that the whole creation has been groaning in travail together until now; [23]and not only the creation, but we ourselves, who have the first fruits of the Spirit, groan inwardly as we wait for adoption as sons, the redemption of our bodies." All creatures – human beings and other creation – have been waiting for Christ's return on the Lord's day. Why? When Christ Jesus returns to us, human beings and other creation will be liberated from their current destiny of corruption. Then, we, both human beings and other creation – the fish of the sea, the birds of the air, the animals, trees and vegetables of the ground – will have eternal life.

All the environmental problems will be gone in the new heaven and the new earth. John in Revelation 21:1-4 and 22:1-5 describes how the new world will look like. The new heaven and the new earth – the restored paradise – obviously is the place where there will be no tears, no pain, no death (Revelation 21:4), but the tree of life bears abundant fruit (Revelation 22:2) in the new paradise. All God's creation will live forever without worrying about the environmental problems. Until then, we can slow down the environmental problems by considering other people and other creation.

# PART III

# THE ECONOMY OF EVANGELISM:

# INTERNATIONAL ECONOMIC ASPECTS

## Chapter Eighteen

# What Is the Economy of Evangelism?

### Another Meaning of *Oikonomia*

As we discussed in Chapter 1, *oikonomia* (economy) also means "mission or dispensation (of spreading or preaching the gospel)" (1 Corinthians 9:17; Ephesians 3:2; Colossians 1:25). Paul in 1 Corinthians 9:17-18 states: "If I do this of my own will, I have a reward; but if not of my own will, I am entrusted with a commission. What then is my reward? Just this: that in my preaching I may make the gospel free of charge, not making full use of my right in the gospel." Paul in Colossians 1:25 speaks of his apostleship (of spreading the good news to the Gentiles) and regards it as "the divine office" that was given to him. The word apostle means 'the one who is sent' and every time Paul mentions his apostleship, he reminds of his duty/mission of spreading the gospel to the Gentiles. Paul uses the word, *oikonomia* (economy), in defining his mission or commission of spreading the gospel to the Gentiles, believing that his mission of spreading the good news is to bring people to God for them to be saved.

### Evangelism

Evangelism is an act of spreading the gospel – good news – to others. The gospel in Greek is εὐαγγέλιον (euanggelion), the compound word of εὐ (good) and αγγέλιον (news). Thayer's Greek Lexicon defines it as 1. a reward for good tidings; and 2. good tidings (2 Samuel 18:20 & 22). The word εὐαγγέλιον (euanggelion) occurs 76 times in the New Testament.

The verb form of εὐαγγέλιον (euanggelion) is εὐαγγελίζω (euanggelizó), which means 'announce good news', 'bring good news,' 'preach good tidings.' The word εὐαγγελίζω (euanggelizó) occurs 61 times in the

New Testament, many times in Luke's books – the Gospel of Luke and Acts.

What is the gospel about? The gospel – good news – is about the Kingdom of Heaven and God's salvation plan through Jesus Christ. In New Testament times, Jesus was the first person who spread the gospel by teaching/preaching about the Kingdom of God during his public ministry and even after his resurrection.

## The Economy of Evangelism in the Gospels

Mark, the author of the Gospel of Mark begins his book with this statement: "The beginning of the gospel of Jesus Christ, the son of God." (Mark 1:1) The core of the four Gospels is the gospel of Jesus Christ, that is, Jesus' proclamation of the kingdom of God. Matthew 4:23 states: "And he (=Jesus) went about all Galilee, teaching in their synagogues and preaching the gospel of the kingdom and healing every disease and every infirmity among the people." As we can see here, the gospel (good news) is about the kingdom of God. Jesus began his preaching of the gospel even before he called his disciples.

Matthew 9:35 states: "And Jesus went about all the cities and villages, teaching in their synagogues and preaching the gospel of the kingdom, and healing every disease and every infirmity." This is the scene of about the middle of Jesus' three-plus-year public ministry. He consistently preached the gospel of the kingdom. Jesus mentioned more laborers of the gospel would be needed here: "[37b]The harvest is plentiful, but the laborers are few; [38]pray therefore the Lord of the harvest to send out laborers into his harvest." (Matthew 9:37-38) When Jesus called his disciples, he wanted to make them to be fishermen of people (cf. Luke 4:10)

Jesus in Matthew 11:4-6 describes his ministry of preaching the gospel, when John the Baptist sent his disciples to him: "[4]Go back and report to John what you hear and see: [5]The blind receive sight, the lame walk, those who have leprosy are cleansed, the deaf hear, the dead are raised, and the good news is proclaimed to the poor. [6]Blessed is anyone who does not stumble on account of me."

Jesus enters a synagogue at Nazareth on the Sabbath day and reads the book of Isaiah, which prophesied about the good news: "[18]The Spirit of the Lord is upon me, because he has anointed me to preach good news to the poor. He has sent me to proclaim release to the captives and recovering of sight to the blind, to set at liberty those who are oppressed, [19]to proclaim the acceptable year of the Lord." (Luke 4:18-19, Isaiah 61:1-2)

Jesus in Matthew 24:14 still talks about the gospel: "And this gospel of the kingdom will be preached throughout the whole world, as a testimony to all nations; and then the end will come." (also, Mark 13:10) Jesus foretold that the gospel would continue to be preached/spread throughout the whole world, knowing that his death was near. According to Jesus, the end (eschaton) will come after the gospel is preached throughout the whole world. Paul states this in Romans 11:25: "I want you to understand this mystery, brethren: a hardening has come upon part of Israel, until the full number of the Gentiles come in" So, the gospel continued to be preached by Jesus' disciples in Jerusalem, Judea and Samaria, and be expanded to the end of the earth. Peter in Acts 15:7 states: "Brethren, you know that in the early days God made choice among you, that by my mouth the Gentiles should hear the word of the gospel and believe. …"

Jesus in Matthew 28:19-20 commands his disciples: "[19]Go therefore and make disciples of all nations, baptizing them in the name of the Father and of the Son and of the Holy Spirit, [20]teaching them to observe all that I have commanded you; and lo, I am with you always, to the close of the age." Mark's version in 16:15-18 is: "[15]Go into all the world and preach the gospel to the whole creation. [16]He who believes and is baptized will be saved; but he who does not believe will be condemned. [17]And these signs will accompany those who believe: in my name they will cast out demons; they will speak in new tongues; [18]they will pick up serpents, and if they drink any deadly thing, it will not hurt them; they will lay their hands on the sick, and they will recover." Again, Jesus in Acts 1:8 commands his disciples: "But you shall receive power when the Holy Spirit has come upon you; and you shall be my witnesses in Jerusalem and in all Judea and Samaria and to the end of the earth." This command in Acts 1:8 may be a different Luke's version of the one in Matthew 28:19-20.

## The Economy of Evangelism in Acts and Paul's Letters

The apostles in the early church does not cease preaching the gospel. Acts 5:42 states: "And every day in the temple and at home they did not cease teaching and preaching Jesus as the Christ." There was a great persecution against the church in Jerusalem (Acts 8:1). So, Christians were all scattered throughout the region of Judea and Samaria, except the apostles. Why did God let his church be persecuted? The persecution of the church was probably the will of God so that the gospel could be heard not only in Jerusalem but also in Judea and Samaria (refer to Acts 1:8)

There was more persecution against the church in Jerusalem (Acts 12). James, brother of John and one of the three primary apostles, was beheaded by Herod the king, and Peter was imprisoned. He later was delivered from prison by the angel of God. The continued persecution of the church in Jerusalem made Christians scattered all over the world. However, this was not only the bad news to the church of God, but it became an opportunity for the church to spread the good news to the end of this earth. When Paul wrote a letter to the people in Rome, those readers of Paul's letter were already Christians although the Bible does not describe how they became Christians. They probably heard the gospel by unknown Christian teachers/preachers.

Paul in Acts 20:24 shows his firm resolution to preach the gospel at the cost of his life: "But I do not account my life of any value nor as precious to myself, if only I may accomplish my course and the ministry which I received from the Lord Jesus, to testify to the gospel of the grace of God." Paul in Romans 1:1 describes that he was called to be an apostle for the gospel of God, the gospel concerning his Son, Jesus Christ. Paul in Romans 1:16 proclaims that the gospel is the power of God for salvation to everyone who has faith.

Paul in Romans 10:16 praises preaching of the gospel by citing Isaiah 52:7, "And how can men preach unless they are sent? As it is written, 'How beautiful are the feet of those who preach good news!'" Paul in Romans 16:25 calls the message he proclaims about Jesus Christ 'my gospel', which was hidden for long ages past but now is revealed and made known.

Paul had founded several churches in Asia Minor, Macedonia, and Achaia. The church at Corinth was one of those churches Paul had founded. Paul in 1 Corinthians 4:15 explains how his relationship with people at the church in Corinth was established: "Even if you had ten thousand guardians in Christ, you do not have many fathers, for in Christ Jesus I became your father through the gospel." The economy of evangelism is an expansion of the economy of God or God's household. Through evangelism more people come to God and enter the household of God – the Kingdom of God.

## Chapter Nineteen

# The Role of the Church in Evangelism

### The Etymology of Church

The word, church, is originally from the Greek word, κύριος (kirios, Lord). The church in German is Kirche and in old English is cirice, meaning the place that belongs to the Lord. The word, ecclesia, which also means church, is from the Greek word, ἐκκλησία (ekklésia). The Greek word, ἐκκλησία is a compound word of ἐκ (ek, out from) and καλέω (kaleo, call) – call out of, and occurs 114 times in the New Testament. According to Thayer's Greek Lexicon, ἐκκλησία (ekklésia), in the Christian sense, means 1. an assembly of Christians gathered for worship; and 2. a company of Christians, or of those who, hoping for eternal salvation through Jesus Christ, observe their own religious rites, hold their own religious meetings, and manage their own affairs according to regulations prescribed for the body for order's sake.[57]

### The Church in the Gospels and Acts

Jesus mentions his church first in Matthew 16:18 when Peter answers him, "You are the Christ, the Son of the living God" (Matthew 16:16): "And I tell you, you are Peter, and on this rock I will build my church, and the powers of death (=the gates of Hades, NIV) shall not prevail against it." Peter's old name was Simon, and Peter which means "rock" was probably named by Jesus.

Jesus says in Matthew 18:17: "If he refuses to listen to them, tell it to the church; and if he refuses to listen even to the church, let him be to you as a Gentile and a tax collector." What church was this in this verse when Jesus' church did not start yet? Jesus probably foretold what the roles of his church would be. Or Jesus and his disciples' gathering was

[57] Thayer's Greek Lexicon. "1577. ἐκκλησία," *BibleHub*. Retrieved from https://biblehub.com/str/greek/1577.htm

already a church although they did not call their assembly "the church" yet.

The first church that was formed after Jesus went up to heaven was the gathering of the 120 disciples at Mary's house in Jerusalem (Acts 1:12-17). And they selected Matthias by casting lots as a new apostle who replaced Judas Iscariot and added to the eleven apostles. They remember what Jesus commanded them while he was still with them in Acts 1:8: "But you shall receive power when the Holy Spirit has come upon you; and you shall be my witnesses in Jerusalem and in all Judea and Samaria and to the end of the earth." So, they stayed together at one place and prayed hard. On the day of Pentecost, as Jesus foretold, the Holy Spirit has come upon the disciples like the rush of a mighty wind and tongues of fire, and they were all filled with the Holy Spirit, speaking in other tongues (Acts 2:1-4). Peter boldly witnessed Jesus Christ and the kingdom of God (Acts 2:14-41). Three thousand people were added to their number on the day when Peter witnessed Jesus Christ (Acts 2:41). According to Acts 2:46, every day they continued to meet together in the temple courts. Acts 4:4 describes another addition of five thousand people. The church in Jerusalem grew so big.

The church in Jerusalem continued to grow. However, the work of the church was limited – prayer and preaching of God's word and daily distribution of food – only in Jerusalem (Acts 6:1-4). In addition to the twelve apostles, the church chose seven men who were known to be full of the Spirit and wisdom (Acts 6:3). They chose Stephen, Philip, Procorus, Nicanor, Timon, Parmenas, and Nicolas from Antioch (Acts 6:5-6). Their primary responsibility was to distribute daily food. However, later they were more known for their witnessing Jesus Christ, spreading the gospel. The number of disciples in Jerusalem increased rapidly (Acts 6:7).

What is the most important mission or role of the church? Jesus already told his disciples and us: "You will be my witnesses in Jerusalem, in Judea and Samaria, and to the end of the earth." – spreading the gospel from near to far, beyond the boundary. Stephen was the first martyr, a true witness (μάρτυς or μάρτυρ) of Jesus Christ (Acts 6:8-7:60). Stephen's martyrdom was a signal or starting point of the church being scattered. Saul was the initiator of the persecution of the church in Jerusalem. Acts 8:3 states: "But Saul was ravaging the church, and entering house after house, he dragged off men and women and committed them to prison." We cannot fathom God's plan and his work. Saul and other persecutors tried to destroy the church of Christ in Jerusalem and human plan of destroying God's church seemed to be successful. People except the apostles were scattered throughout Judea and Samaria (Acts 8:1-3). How amazing God's plan or work is! If the Church had remained only in Jerusalem, there would have been no more fruit outside Jerusalem. People at the church in Jerusalem did not want to leave Jerusalem. God forcefully scattered people at the church in Jerusalem, using Saul the persecutor. This was for the expansion of God's economy – his saving plan of his people.

Philip, one of the seven who were chosen in Acts 6, spread the gospel in Samaria (Acts 8:5-13). He proclaimed the gospel about the kingdom of God and Jesus Christ to people in Samaria, performed miraculous signs, healed the sick people, and baptized people there. There was a man called Simon the sorcerer among those who were baptized by Philip. He followed Philip everywhere, astonished by the great signs and miracles that he saw (Acts 8:13). This Simon Magus, the magician or sorcerer, wanted to buy the power of the Holy Spirit with money, asking Peter later when he visited Samaria. Simon said to Peter and John in Acts 8:19: "Give me also this power, that any one on whom I lay my hands may receive the Holy Spirit." Peter answered to him in Acts 8:20: "Your silver perish with you, because you thought you could obtain the gift of God with money!" Simon Magus later was known for the founder of Gnosticism, a heretical movement of the second century gnostic church. This name Simon Magus is very important in the study of heresy in the second and third centuries. More seriously, his name – Simon Magus – was used in the fight between the Jewish Christianity that was centered in Rome and the Gentile Christianity that was in centered in Asia Minor and other areas that Paul had traveled and founded his churches. We can see a hint of this later fight even in Acts 15, the debate between the Jewish Christians and Paul and Barnabas, representing their gospel for the Gentiles. The Jewish Christians insist that people are required to have faith in Jesus, and be baptized and observe Moses' law, including the dietary law whereas

Paul claims that people, whether the Jews or the Gentiles, only need to have faith in Jesus Christ. This early debate did not go too far, separation between the Jewish Christians (the church in Rome) and the Gentile Christians (the churches in Asia Minor) as James and Peter intervened in the debate and resolved the issue. However, later during the second century to the fourth century, the Jewish Christians in Rome persecuted the Gentile Christians in Asia Minor, claiming that their Christianity was heresy. The Jewish Christians used Simon in Acts 8, claiming that this Simon is no other than Paul in disguise. The second century pseudo-Clementine literature and other New Testament apocryphal books deal with the confrontation between Peter and Simon, Paul in disguise, whose theme was derived from Acts 8, the conversation between Simon and Peter.

Philip continued to spread the gospel further even to an Ethiopian eunuch, an important official who was in charge of all the treasury of the queen of the Ethiopians (Acts 9:26-39). He interpreted the Scripture verses that the eunuch was reading (Isaiah 53:7-8) and let him understand the meaning of the verses. The eunuch wanted to be baptized and became a Christian. According to the tradition, this eunuch went back to Ethiopia and spread the gospel there. And this is the beginning of evangelism in Africa. Philip further spread the gospel in Azotus, other towns until he reached Caesarea (Acts 8:40).

God's amazing and mysterious plan was revealed in Acts 9, changing Saul the persecutor to Paul the persecutee. Saul was heading for Damascus to take the believers as prisoners to Jerusalem (Acts 9:2). Then, what happened to him? He encountered Jesus who appeared to him in the form of light (Acts 9:3-19; 22:6-16; and 26:9-23). Jesus called Paul to make him an apostle to the Gentiles (Acts 9:15). Paul preached the gospel in Damascus, instead of catching the believers there (Acts 9:20-22). As we saw in Chapter 17, Peter, according to God's plan, was sent to Cornelius' house to spread the gospel to a Gentile family (Acts 10).

People who were scattered by the persecution in Acts 8 traveled as far as Phoenicia, Cyprus and Antioch, spreading the gospel only among Jews (Acts 11:19). Barnabas visited Paul who was staying at Tarsus and brought him to Antioch, where they taught the word of God for a full year. And the disciples were called Christians first at Antioch (Acts 11:25-26). Paul's ministry at Antioch played an important role in establishing his experience at Damascus theologically and providing the basic structure for his coming mission trips to towns in Asia Minor, Macedonia, and Achaia. The church at Antioch was very important as it was a base that dispatched Paul and Barnabas as missionaries for the first time.

God did not let his church remain stable for a long time. He shook it again more strongly. As we saw in Chapter 17, James, one the primary church leaders, was beheaded by king Herod (Acts 12:1-2). Why did God allow his church to be persecuted? God wanted his church to be scattered further away. Being scattered, God's household could include more people. In the midst of persecutions, God's church did not stop growing and was scattered. Acts 13:1-3 states: "[1]Now in the church at Antioch there were prophets and teachers, Barnabas, Simeon who was called Niger, Lucius of Cyrene, Manaen a member of the court of Herod the tetrarch, and Saul. [2]While they were worshiping the Lord and fasting, the Holy Spirit said, 'Set apart for me Barnabas and Saul for the work to which I have called them.' [3]Then after fasting and praying they laid their hands on them and sent them off." The church at Antioch in Syria dispatched Paul and Barnabas as missionaries to Asia Minor. This was the beginning of sending out missionaries and the reason why Paul was called by Jesus.

## The Church in Paul's Epistles

Paul used the word ecclesia as a particular place for worship and religious education, or a meeting of local Christians, or Christians who belong to Christ as a whole. He probably accepted the existing meaning of ecclesia, "congregation," and developed its meaning as an organic relationship between Christ and his people. Paul calls the church as 'the body of Christ,' Christians as 'members in one body of Christ' (Romans 12; 1 Corinthians 12), and Christ as 'the head of the church' (Ephesians and Colossians), which are the characteristic expressions that can be found only in Paul's epistles.

### 1. The Church as God's People

For Paul, the church (ecclesia) means a congregation of people who believed in Jesus Christ and were baptized into Christ (Romans 6). That is, the church in Paul's epistles can be understood Christians as God's people in the New Testament, like the Israelites as God's people in the Old Testament.

### 2. The Church as the Body of Christ

For Paul, the church (ecclesia) means a congregation of people who believed in Jesus Christ and were baptized into Christ (Romans 6). That is, the church in Paul's epistles can be understood Christians as God's people in the New Testament, like the Israelites as God's people in the Old Testament. Paul in 1 Corinthians 12:27 states: "Now you are the body of Christ and individually members of it." Paul calls the church the body of Christ to express the intimate and united relationship between Jesus Christ and his people. Paul in Ephesians 5:31-32 states: "[31]For this reason a man shall leave his father and mother and be joined to his wife, and the two shall become one flesh. [32]This mystery is a profound one, and I am saying that it refers to Christ and the church." To Paul, the unity of Christ and his people is just like the unity of a man and his wife. Paul in Ephesians 1:22-23 states: "[22]And he (=God) has put all things under his feet and has made him the head over all things for the church, [23]which is his body, the fullness of him who fills all in all." (cf. Colossians 1:18) The church, the body of Christ, will be directed by Jesus Christ.

### 3. The Church as a Local Church

Most early Christian churches in the first century were small. The church building was not available until the third century. The first century churches did not have a building but met at rich people's houses for worship and Holy Communion, which were house churches. To Paul, the unity or group of Christians was more important than a place/building as the meaning of the church. The importance of the church for Paul was not to show its power but to spread the gospel to expand the household of God. For Paul, the church is a foundation or a place that can initiate spreading the gospel and/or sharing the richer people's possessions with the poorer people to perform the economics of equality.

## The Role of the Church Today

What is the role of the church today? From the early church till the church today, the most important role of the church is not to build a large building or buy land but to spread the gospel – kingdom of God and salvation through Jesus Christ – in Jerusalem, Judea and Samaria, and to the end of this earth.

## Chapter Twenty

# Expansion of God's Household

### God's Household

Who belonged to God's household in the beginning of this world? Genesis 1:27 states: "So God created mankind (אָדָם, adam) in his own image, in the image of God he created them; male (זָכָר, zakar) and female (נְקֵבָה, neqebah) he created them." A man (Adam, אָדָם) and a woman (Eve, חַוָּה) were those two who belonged to God's household as God had created them and placed them in his garden. Those people who belong to God's household are the ones that are taken care of by God. When Adam and Eve fell, they were expelled from the garden of Eden and nobody belonged to God's household. Thereafter, God's relationship with mankind became individual.

### Expansion of God's Household in the Old Testament

Enoch faithfully walked with God (Genesis 5:22, 24), and God took him away (to heaven) (Genesis 5:24). So, Enoch belonged to God's household although there was no physical place for God's household any longer. Noah faithfully walked with God (Genesis 6:9), and so he belonged to God's household. Not only Noah but also his wife, his sons – Shem, Ham, and Japheth – and their wives belonged to God's household. God takes care of people who belong to his household and blesses them. It is the economy of God – God's economic and political governing activities for his people.

Then, Abraham, Isaac, Jacob, Joseph, and their families belonged to God's household. God continuously appeared to them, making sure that his promises and blessings would surely be fulfilled. While Joseph was a prime minister of Egypt, Jacob, his sons, and other family members moved to the land of Egypt. The total number of Jacob's family members who went to Egypt was about 70 according to Genesis 46:27 or 75 according to Acts 7:14 (which followed Septuagint, the

Greek translation of the Hebrew Scriptures). So, God's household expanded to around 70 people when Jacob and his family settled in Egypt.

The Israelites stayed in Egypt for 400 years (Genesis 15:13; Acts 7:6) or 430 years (Exodus 12:40-41; Galatians 3:17) until God called Moses to lead them out of Egypt. The number of men (of the Israelites) who were twenty years old or more and able to serve in the army was 603,550 when God told Moses to number on the first day of the second month of the second year after the Israelites came out of Egypt (Numbers 1:1-46). So, the total number of the Israelites, including all women, children, and old people, was probably 2-3 million. So, God's household was no longer a small size. However, God wanted his household to grow, including not only the Israelites but also the Gentiles later when the opportune time would come.

God in Isaiah 45:22 calls all nations: "Turn to me and be saved, all the ends of the earth! For I am God, and there is no other." There is only one God in whom there is salvation. Isaiah 52:7 states: "How beautiful upon the mountains are the feet of him who brings good tidings, who publishes peace, who brings good tidings of good, who publishes salvation, who says to Zion, 'Your God reigns.'" God encourages and praises those who spread the good news although this is yet to be realized in the future. God through Isaiah in Isaiah 54:2-3 proclaims: "[2]Enlarge the place of your tent and let the curtains of your habitations be stretched out; hold not back, lengthen your cords and strengthen your stakes. [3]For you will spread abroad to the right and to the left, and your descendants will possess the nations and will people the desolate cities." God wants us to expand his household in all directions so that more people can dwell in his tent/household. God in Isaiah 55:1 invites people: "Ho, everyone who thirsts, come to the waters; and he who has no money, come, buy and eat! Come, buy wine and milk without money and without price." Expansion of God's household or kingdom is not construction of larger church buildings. It is spreading the gospel to more people and more nations to bring them to his household as there is life in him.

## Expansion of God's Household in the New Testament

When the opportune time arrived, Jesus Christ came to his people to proclaim the gospel. The real good news is that God's salvation is not only for the Jews but also for the Gentiles, including all people whom God had created. Jesus in John 3:16 proclaims: "For God so loved the world that he gave his only Son, that whoever believes in him should not perish but have eternal life." However, Jesus was aware of his limited resources with human flesh. When a Canaanite woman asked him to heal her demon-possessed daughter, Jesus answered in Matthew 15:24: "I was sent only to the lost sheep of the house of Israel." Jesus in Matthew 10:5-6 tells his disciples: "[5]Go nowhere among the Gentiles, and enter no town of the Samaritans, [6]but go rather to the lost sheep of the house of Israel." What does this mean? Why did Jesus prohibited his disciples from going to the Samaritans or the Gentiles? It is a matter of order in spreading the gospel. Spreading the gospel should be in Jerusalem first; then in Judea, and Samaria; and then to the ends of the earth (Acts 1:8). Jesus' disciples had to wait for the Holy Spirit to go beyond Jerusalem to the ends of the earth as the Holy Spirit has no limitation in time and space and can be present everywhere and

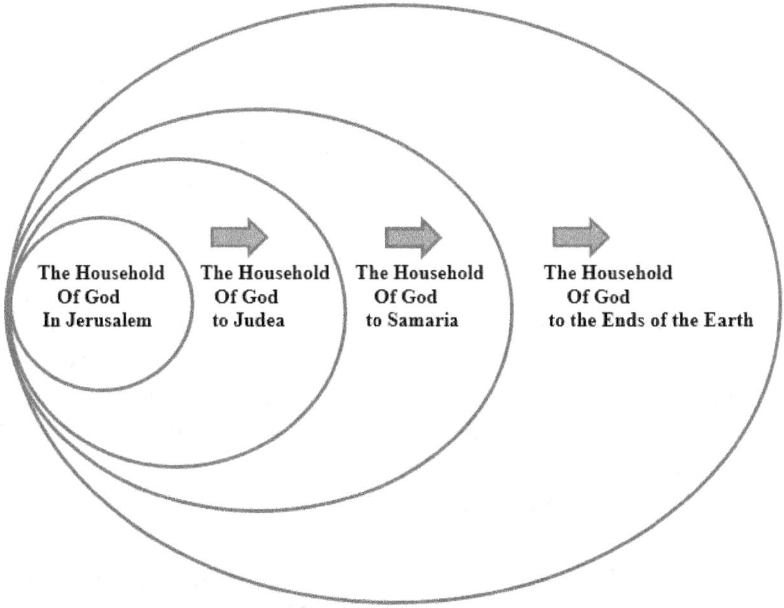


**Expansion of the Household of God**

Jesus in Matthew 28:19-20 tells his disciples: "[19]Go therefore and make disciples of all nations, baptizing them in the name of the Father and of the Son and of the Holy Spirit, [20]teaching them to observe all that I have commanded you; and lo, I am with you always, to the close of the age." As we reviewed in Chapter 19, the gospel was proclaimed in Jerusalem (Acts 2-7), then in Judea and Samaria (Acts 8), and was scattered further away (Acts 12-28).

Jesus called Saul who persecuted his church – the body of Christ. Why? Jesus tells Ananias about Saul/Paul in Acts 9:15-16 (also Acts 22:21, 26:17): "[15]Go, for he is a chosen instrument of mine to carry my name before the Gentiles and kings and the sons of Israel; [16]for I will show him how much he must suffer for the sake of my name." How excited it was! Saul who persecuted Christians in Jerusalem and was going to Damascus to persecute more Christians became Paul who would be persecuted for Christ's sake.

Paul uses the word, *oikonomia* (economy), in defining his mission or commission of spreading the gospel to the Gentiles, believing that his mission of spreading the good news is to bring more people to God for them to be saved. Paul's economy or mission is to spread the gospel to the ends of the earth, expanding God's household. Paul in 1 Corinthians 9:17-18 states: "If I do this of my own will, I have a reward; but if not of my own will, I am entrusted with a commission. What then is my reward? Just this: that in my preaching I may make the gospel free of charge, not making full use of my right in the gospel." Paul in Ephesians 3:2 calls his mission to preach the good news to the Gentiles, including the people in Ephesus, "the stewardship (or commission, NRSV) of God's grace" that was given to him for the Gentiles. Paul regards his mission or stewardship (of spreading the gospel to the Gentiles) as "God's grace and gift." Paul in Colossians 1:25 speaks of his apostleship (of spreading the good news to the Gentiles) and regards it as "the divine office" that was given to him. The word apostle means 'the one who is sent' and every time Paul mentions his apostleship, he reminds of his duty/mission of spreading the gospel to the Gentiles.

Why did Paul want to be sent to Rome when he was caught in Jerusalem (Acts 25:10-12)? When Paul was going to Jerusalem during his third missionary journey, he already had a plan to go to Spain, where he thought was the end of the earth (Romans 15:28). He wanted to make a good use of this unfortunate incidence. He was seeking an opportunity to spread the gospel to the ends of the earth. When Paul arrived at Rome, he was allowed to live by himself, with a soldier to guard him (Acts 28:16). Paul in Acts 28:28 states: "Let it be known to you then that this salvation of God has been sent to the Gentiles; they will listen." Paul stayed in his own rented house in Rome for two full years and taught the kingdom of God and Jesus Christ. Paul's journey of Christian life was about to end. 2 Timothy is kind of Paul's last word to his beloved brother or son in Christ, Timothy. He charges Timothy to preach the Word of God in season and out of season, that is whether the time is favorable or unfavorable (2 Timothy 4:2). We should spread the Good News not only when the time is favorable for us but also when the time is unfavorable.

### Expansion of God's Household by Numerous Christians

God's household continues to be expanded through many Christians, including Paul, Peter, John, James, Stephen, Philip, and many other known and unknown Christians. According to the New Testament apocrypha and other traditions, Paul was beheaded in Rome, Peter was crucified upside down in Rome, and Thomas went to India and was killed there, and many other unknown Christians spread the gospel and died for Christ's name.

In the early church period, those Christians who were in Rome lived together in a catacomb, which was an underground public cemetery. They lived a communal life there, escaping from the lookout of the Roman government. The Christians in Rome praised God and worshipped Him there. Although there were neither gracious hymns nor the holy Bible yet, they praised the suffering, death, and resurrection of Jesus for the salvation of human beings. They enjoyed those hours of singing and praying. Some of them were from rich families, but they gave up all things and joined other Christians in the communal life in a catacomb as they regarded the life of following and witnessing Jesus as the most valuable matter. Some wall paintings were found in the catacombs. The paintings were about Jesus' last supper with his disciples and the resurrected Jesus. They longed to see Jesus very much.

Polycarp, bishop of the church in Smyrna in the second century was caught and brought to the proconsul to be martyred.[58] But, seeing Polycarp's old age, the proconsul told him: "Respect your age. Swear by the genius of Caesar, repent, say: 'Away with the Atheists.'" Polycarp was silent for a while. The proconsul pressed him, saying: "Take the oath and I will let you go. Revile Christ!" Then, Polycarp answered: "For eighty-six years have I been his servant, and he has done me nothing wrong, and how can I blaspheme my King who saved me." The proconsul persisted again, saying: "Swear by the genius of Caesar!" Polycarp answered: "If you vainly suppose that I will swear by the genius of Caesar, as you say, and pretend that you are ignorant who I am, listen plainly: I am a Christian. And if you wish to learn the doctrine of Christianity, fix a day and listen." The proconsul said: "I have wild beasts, I will deliver you to them, unless you repent." Polycarp answered: "Call for them, for repentance from better to worse is not allowed to us; but it is good to change from evil to righteousness." The proconsul said: "I will cause you to be consumed by fire, if you despise the beasts, unless you repent." Polycarp responded: "You threaten with fire that burns for a time, and is quickly quenched, for you do not know the fire which awaits the wicked in the judgment to come and in everlasting punishment. But why are you waiting? Come, do what you will." Polycarp was so brave before death, as he was so sure about what would wait for him.

In a novel, *Silence*, written by a Japanese novelist, Shusaku Endo, there is an inspirational story of a Portuguese Catholic priest, Francisco Garrpe. [59] Although Japanese officials kept commanding him to apostatize, he rejected their enforcement. He did not deny Jesus Christ. He was tied on the post at the shore of the sea where the tide kept coming in. Garrpe was singing and praying to God even until the water sank him to the neck. Finally, the head of Garrpe was lost in the sea but the voice was still there.

---

[58] Eusebius, *The Ecclesiastical History*, Grand Rapids, MI: Baker Book House, 1993.
[59] Shusaku Endo, Silence. Picador Modern Classics, 2016.

There was an American missionary named Adoniram Judson (1788-1850) in the early 19th century in Burma. He spread the good news diligently there for almost six years but could not bear any fruit. Yet, he did not lose his confidence, believing "As God has sent me here, He will let me bear the fruit of evangelism." He continued to witness Jesus Christ to the people living there. And finally, he earned a person who decided to accept Jesus as his personal Savior. Judson baptized him in the name of the Father, of the Son, and of the Holy Spirit. He was the first fruit in that land as a result of Judson's efforts of six years. However, one century later, there were more than fifty thousand believers there. When we witness Jesus, we don't have to worry about the result. We just plant the seed of the good news and water, then God gave the growth (cf. 1 Cor. 3:6).

There was a famous Scotch athlete who also had the same rule of life with that of Jonathan Edwards. His name was Eric Liddell (1902-1945) who participated in 1924 Paris Olympics. He was a world record holder in four-hundred-meter dash. But, as the final was held on Sunday, he declined to participate in the event. The prime minister of Scotland called him to urge him to participate in the race for the glory of his country Scotland. But his decision was not changed. The dream of amateur athletes is to earn a gold medal in an Olympic final. However, Eric Liddell gave up his dream of gold medal to live by his rule of life. Eric Liddell thought that "spreading the gospel is every believer's mission." Thus, he as a believer decided to spread the gospel. He became a missionary and went to China to live by his rule of life as a Christian. His life as a missionary was sometimes painful and poor, but he was very happy and glad as he lived according to his rule of life which was truthful to God. His biography was published as a book and its title was "The Flying Scotchman." Later, it was made into a movie and its title was "Chariots of Fire." Elijah in the Bible rode the chariots of fire to go up to heaven alive. Eric Liddell liked the great prophet Elijah and tried to live by the Word of God.

Jesus Christ is a good example of a missionary. Jesus was a missionary who was sent out by God the Father from the heavenly country down to the earthly country. First of all, as a missionary who was dispatched down to the earthly country, Jesus took off his heavenly glorious clothes and wore the earthly clothes, that is, a human flesh. As a missionary Jesus wanted to be like one of the earthly people. He wanted to expand God's household on earth. Spreading the gospel is the most important mission to anybody who wants to be a disciple of Jesus. Thus, we, the followers of Jesus, should not abandon the opportunities that are given by God. John Scott, a famous biblical scholar and pastor, points out in his book, 「Guilty Silence」 , that "if anyone is silent without telling the gospel to a neighbor who is dying without knowing Jesus Christ, he is guilty of not telling the truth."

# PART IV

# CHRISTIAN ECONOMIC ETHICS:

# ETHICAL ECONOMIC ASPECTS

Chapter Twenty-One

# What Is Christian Economic Ethics?

## Ethical Issues in the Real Business World

In economics, some ethical problems arise due to adverse selection and moral hazard. Adverse selection is related to dishonesty under information asymmetry whereas moral hazard is related to self-indulgence or a lavish life style. The 2008-2009 financial crisis was caused not only by the housing market bubble but also more importantly by people's moral hazard problems and/or business people's unethical ways of life. Commercial banks and other financial institutions invested their customers' money on very risky housing market-related securities – MBS (mortgage-backed security), CDOs (collateralized debt obligations), CMOs (collateralized mortgage obligations), etc. When the housing market was booming, they could earn a lot of profits/dividends. They enjoyed profits in the form of bonuses and stock options among themselves with other people's money. When the housing market began to go down in 2017 and collapsed in 2018, some went bankrupt and some others were in danger of bankrupt. The government provided them relief fund to activate the economy by letting them lend more money to corporations and people. However, instead of lending money to the needed corporations and investors, they enjoyed bonuses and pay raise among themselves with the money that was provided by the government – tax payers' money. This was a typical example of a moral hazard problem or a problem of economic or business ethics.

## Characteristics of Christian Economic Ethics

If you misunderstand the Bible, especially Jesus and Paul, you may think that you are free from all the restrictions as you are saved by faith in Jesus Christ through the grace of God. Some people think they may be okay even though their life is unethical as they were already saved. However, Christian freedom is different from self-indulgence.

What are ethical behaviors and unethical behaviors in terms of economic or business ethics? Poverty or wealth itself does not tell whether the person is ethical or unethical. Some people work hard, honestly and diligently but are still poor whereas some other people do not work hard yet are rich by exploiting their employees or cheating other people. There are some poor people as they are lazy whereas some other people are wealthy as they work diligently. O. C. Ferrell, J. Fraedrich, and L. Ferrell list integrity, honesty, and fairness as the foundational values for identifying ethical issues.[60] What are Christian values or standards for economic or business ethics that you can find in the Bible?

## 1. Honesty

Believers should be honest or just in their business, not deceiving their clients. God in Leviticus 19:36 tells the Israelites: "Use <u>honest</u> scales and <u>honest</u> weights, an <u>honest</u> ephah and an <u>honest</u> (= just, RSV) hin. I am the Lord your God, who brought you out of Egypt" (NIV). Moses (or God through Moses) in Deuteronomy 25:13-16 also emphasizes honesty: "You shall not have in your bag two kinds of weights, a large and a small. [14]You shall not have in your house two kinds of measures, a large and a small. [15]A full and just weight you shall have, a full and just measure you shall have; that your days may be prolonged in the land which the Lord your God gives you. [16]For all who do such things, all who act dishonestly, are an abomination to the Lord your God." Proverbs 13:11 states: "Dishonest money dwindles away, but whoever gathers money little by little makes it grow" (NIV). The old saying or Benjamin Franklin states, "Honesty is the best policy." When your clients recognize that you are an honest business person, they will refer you to their family members, relatives, and friends.

## 2. Integrity

Economic ethics also asks for integrity not crookedness. Proverbs 11:3 states: "The integrity of the upright (or honesty, NLT) guides them, but the crookedness of the treacherous (or dishonesty, NLT) destroys them." And Proverbs 19:1 states: "Better is a poor man who walks in

---

[60] O. C. Ferrell, J. Fraedrich, L. Ferrell, *Business Ethics: Ethical Decision Making and Cases* (12th ed.), Cengage Learning, 2019, 58-60.

his integrity (or blameless, NIV) than a man who is perverse in speech and is a fool." Integrity is directly related with honesty whereas crookedness with dishonesty.

### 3. Fairness or Impartiality

Fairness or impartiality may go along with honesty, which is also a very much important characteristic of God. Deuteronomy 10:17 states: "For the Lord your God is God of gods and Lord of lords, the great, the mighty, and the terrible God, who is not partial and takes no bribe." When you are fair or impartial as a business person, you do not take any bribe and do not show any favoritism. Paul in Romans 2:11 acknowledges God's fairness: "For God shows no partiality." As God shows impartiality or fairness, we, the people of God, show also show fairness or impartiality in our life.**Humility**

A humble heart not arrogance is required for good business or economic ethics. As a business owner or entrepreneur, you must be humble not arrogant when you deal with your employees. They will respect you and work hard. James in James 4:10 advises us: "Humble yourselves before the Lord and he will exalt you." Peter in 1 Peter 5:5 says: "Likewise you that are younger be subject to the elders. Clothe yourselves, all of you, with humility toward one another, for 'God opposes the proud, but gives grace to the humble.'" Jesus in Luke 14:11 states: "For everyone who exalts himself will be humbled, and he who humbles himself will be exalted." Jesus shows an example of self-humility when he came down to earth with human flesh and lived a life on the earth. Paul in Philippians 2:5-11 describes Jesus' humble life, total obedience to God the Father unto death on cross. Then, God exalted him to the highest place.

### 4. Modesty

Economic ethics asks for a modest life not an extravagant or lavish life. Proverbs 15:16 states: "Better a little with the fear of the Lord than great treasure (or wealth, NIV) and trouble with it." Business or economic ethical issues often occur when people want to live a luxurious life that they cannot afford to maintain. They may owe money due to their lavish lifestyle and thus they seek unlawful ways to make more money. Christians also live their life according to the Spirit not according to their fleshly desires. Paul in Galatians 5:16-17 advises us: "[16]But I say, walk by the Spirit, and do not gratify the desires of the flesh. [17]For the desires of the flesh are against the Spirit, and the desires of the Spirit are against the flesh; for these are opposed to each other, to prevent you from doing what you would." God's people try to live a modest life not only materially but also spiritually.

### 5. Not Too Much Greed

Greed is a part of human nature. Greed to a certain extent may make people work hard. However, too much greed makes people become unethical. Proverbs 28:25 states: "A greedy man stirs up strife, but he who trusts in the Lord will be enriched." Ecclesiastes 5:10 states: "He who loves money will not be satisfied with money; nor he who loves wealth, with gain: this also is vanity." A man's greed can never be satisfied, and it makes him away from God. He will be too busy in making money to seek God. Greedy mind may accept bribes. Proverbs 15:27 states: "He who is greedy for unjust gain makes trouble for his household, but he who hates bribes will live." Jesus in Luke 12:15 says: "Take heed and beware of all covetousness (or greed, NIV); for a man's life does not consist in the abundance of his possessions."

### 6. Diligence

Economic ethics asks you to be diligent not lazy. Proverbs 12:24 states: "The hand of the diligent will rule, while the slothful will be put to forced labor." Proverbs 13:4 states: "The soul of the sluggard craves, and gets nothing, while the soul of the diligent is richly supplied." Peter in 2 Peter 1:10 states: "Therefore, brethren, be the more zealous (or diligent, ESV) to confirm your call and election, for if you do this you will never fall." As we previously discussed, poverty due to laziness is not God's blessing and cannot get God's commend. In Jesus' parable of talents, the servant who was entrusted one talent was lazy in managing his master's money (although the master had an intention to give it along with whatever profit he would make to him). The master rebuked him later as he was economically unethical (Matthew 25:26-27).

### 7. Trustworthiness or Faithfulness

Christian economic ethics requires you to be trustworthy or faithful not unfaithful. Jesus in Luke 16:10 states: "He who is faithful in a very little is faithful also in much; and he who is dishonest in a very little is dishonest also in much." Paul in 1 Corinthians 4:2: "Moreover it is required of stewards that they be found trustworthy (or faithful, NIV)." Each Christian who is entrusted God's property and talents should be trustworthy or faithful.

### 8. Generosity

Generosity not reluctance is another good characteristic to be economically ethical. When you are reluctant or forced to do business, your business conduct may not be ethical. A generous mind will make you a man of good conduct in your business. Paul in 2 Corinthians 9:6-7 states: "[6]The point is this: he who sows sparingly will also reap sparingly, and he who sows bountifully will also reap bountifully (or generously, NIV). [7]Each one must do as he has made up his mind, not reluctantly or under compulsion, for God loves a cheerful giver."

## Christian Freedom and Its Boundary

Jesus Christ, the Truth, set us free (John 8:3). So, believers are no more under the law but under the grace of God. However, it does not mean that their Christian conduct is unbounded. Paul in Romans 6:1-2 states: "[1]What shall we say, then? Are we to continue in sin that grace may abound? [2]By no means! How can we who died to sin still live in it?"

Christian conduct has its boundary – if our conduct is within its boundary, it is ethical; if it goes beyond its boundary, it becomes unethical. Paul in 1 Corinthians 6:12 says: "'All things are lawful for me,' but not all things are helpful. 'All things are lawful for me,' but I will not be enslaved by anything." Although someone may say, 'I have the right to do anything,' his or her conduct should be such that first, it should be beneficial to other people (or should not be harmful to others), and second, it should not be controlled or mastered by anything (or it should be constructive for others and community). Paul in 1 Corinthians 10:23 repeats what he says in 1 Corinthians 6:12: "'All things are lawful,' but not all things are helpful. 'All things are lawful,' but not all things build up." Paul adds there in 1 Corinthians 10:24: "Let no one seek his own good, but the good of his neighbor." When we work for the good of others, our Christian economic ethics can be completed. When I was a college student, I joined a Christian club, JOY, which stands for Jesus, Others, and You – the priority should be in this order in our life. Paul emphasizes the order of a Christian's conduct – Jesus, others, and you.

Paul in 1 Corinthians 8:9 states: "Only take care lest this liberty of yours somehow become a stumbling block to the weak"; then in 1 Corinthians 8:13: "Therefore, if food is a cause of my brother's falling, I will never eat meat, lest I cause my brother to fall." Paul in Romans 14:13 states: "Then let us no more pass judgment on one another, but rather decide never to put a stumbling block or hindrance in the way of a brother." Paul's advice is about a Christian conduct in general, however, we can apply this to Christian economic ethics as it is a way of our daily decision making as a Christian.

## Chapter Twenty-Two

# Economic Ethics in Different Relations

### Individual Ethics in the Bible

As we studied in Chapter 21, to live an ethical life, each individual should be honest (or just), fair, modest, blameless, not too much greedy, humble, generous, diligent, and trustworthy (or faithful). In this chapter, we will review Christians' economic ethics in their relationships with others. Believers should not live according to the habit of this world but according to the word of God as wrongdoers will not inherit the kingdom of God (1 Corinthians 6:9-10; Galatians 5:19-21; Ephesians 5:5) and cannot please God. They should not conform to the pattern of this world but be transformed by renewing their mind (Romans 12:2).

Paul advises believers to avoid lawsuits when there is a debate or a fight among believers (1 Corinthians 6:1-6). Paul in 1 Corinthians 6:7 states: "To have lawsuits at all with one another is defeat for you. Why not rather suffer wrong? Why not rather be defrauded?" As we discussed, the economy of God is God's governing activities and rules over each different unit of his household. So, each household's ethics should be based on God's governing activities and rules.

### Household Ethics in the Bible

#### 1. Husbands and Wives

Paul in 1 Corinthians 7:3-4 states: "[3]The husband should give to his wife her conjugal rights, and likewise the wife to her husband. [4]For the wife does not rule over her own body, but the husband does; likewise, the husband does not rule over his own body, but the wife does." Paul in 1 Corinthians 7:3-4 advises husbands and wives to fulfill their duty to each other. Both husbands and wives should fulfill their duty first, instead of demanding the other's duty.

Paul in Ephesians 5:22-23 and 25 states: "[22]Wives, be subject to your husbands, as to the Lord. [23]For the husband is the head of the wife as Christ is the head of the church, his body, and is himself its Savior. … [25]Husbands, love your wives, as Christ loved the church and gave himself up for her." Paul in Ephesians 5:21-33 compares the relationship between the husband and the wife to the relationship between Christ (the head of the church) and his people (the body of Christ). According to Paul, wives should submit themselves to their husbands as they submit themselves to the Lord whereas husbands should love their wives as Christ loves the church.

### 2. Parents and Children

Paul in Ephesians 6:1-4 advises children and parents: "[1]Children, obey your parents in the Lord, for this is right. [2]Honor your father and mother (this is the first commandment with a promise), [3]that it may be well with you and that you may live long on the earth. [4]Fathers, do not provoke your children to anger, but bring them up in the discipline and instruction of the Lord." Paul in Colossians 3:20-21 also advises children and parents: "[20]Children, obey your parents in everything, for this pleases the Lord. [21]Fathers, do not provoke your children, lest they become discouraged." The relationship between God and his people is parallel with human parents and their children. Children's ethical duty for their parents in Ephesians 6:1-4 and Colossians 3:20-21 does not seem to be Paul's own but is from Exodus 20:12 (also in Deuteronomy 5:16). God in Exodus 20:12 tells the Israelites: "Honor your father and your mother, that your days may be long in the land which the Lord your God gives you." The phrase, "it may be well with you," in Ephesians 6:3a implies God's blessings in quality, and the phrase, "you may live long on the earth," in Ephesians 6:3b implies God's blessings in quantity.[61] "The earth" is "the land of promise" which points to not only the Kingdom of God but also the land where we live today, and God is with us. While God in Exodus 20:12 (Deuteronomy 5:16) tells only children's ethical duty for their parents, Paul in Ephesians 6:1-4 (Colossians 3:20-21) also includes parents'

---

[61] K. P. Choi, *To Me, To Live Is Christ: Oikonomia Bible Interpretation Series 2 – Ephesians-Philippians* (in Korean). Seoul, Korea: Qumran Publishing House, 1999, 173-174.

ethical duty for their children. Children are not parents' property but are the ones that belong to God's household and are entrusted to their parents.

## Church Ethics in the Bible

Paul in 1 Corinthians 12:24b-27 states: "[24b]But God has so composed the body, giving the greater honor to the inferior part, [25]that there may be no discord in the body, but that the members may have the same care for one another. [26]If one member suffers, all suffer together; if one member is honored, all rejoice together." Paul explains the church ethics or the ethical culture that exists among believers in the church. Some believers blame or find fault with others. There may be a division in the church, and sometimes some members bring their debates to the court. Paul advises them that believers are one body of Christ and the parts that belong to the same body. If one part of the body suffers, every part of the same body suffers with it; if one part is honored, every part rejoices with it (1 Corinthians 12:26). As Christians are one body of Christ, so there should be no division or conflicts among themselves.

## Social Ethics in the Bible

Paul in Romans 12:14-21 explains social ethics for believers. First, "Bless those who persecute you; bless and do not curse them" (v. 14). Paul seemed to be aware of Jesus' saying in Matthew 5:44, "love your enemies and pray for those who persecute you." Second, "Rejoice with those who rejoice; weep with those who weep" (v. 15). Those who rejoice and those who mourn here are those outside of the church. Christians should also be sympathetic with unbelievers. Third, "Live in harmony with one another" (v. 16a). Believers do not live separately from unbelievers. So, believers learn how to live, in harmony with others in the same community. Fourth, "Do not be haughty, but associate with the lowly" (v. 16b). This is the example of life that Jesus Christ had shown in this world (Philippians 2:5-8). Fifth, "Never be conceited" (or "Don't think you know it all!", NLT) (v. 16c). Our human wisdom is nothing, comparing with the wisdom of God. Sixth, "Repay no one evil for evil, but take thought for what is noble in the sight of all" (v. 17; see also 1 Peter 3:9). Proverbs 17:13 states: "If a man returns evil for good, evil will not depart from his house." Evil goes against the image of God whereas good follows and imitates the image of God. Seventh, "If possible, so far as it depends upon you, live peaceably with all" (v. 18). Believers should live also at peace with unbelievers so that they may find an opportunity to spread the gospel. Eighth, "Beloved, never avenge yourselves, but leave it to the wrath of God" (v. 19). This is wisdom of believers who live in this world. Otherwise, vengeance will produce another vengeance. Ninth, "If your enemy is hungry, feed him; if he is thirsty, give him drink; for by so doing you will heap burning coals upon his head" (v. 20, Proverbs 25:21-22). This is the ethics of love that can embrace even enemies. Believers good conduct will make an evil person be shameful, and later let them open their heart. Tenth, "Do not be overcome by evil, but overcome evil with good" (v. 21). What God wants believers to do is to build a society where God's goodness is revealed. When believers overcome evil with good, God will let them build the Kingdom of God or God's household on this earth and expand it until the Lord returns to us.

### 1. Neighbors Relation

The second part of Moses' ten commandments (6th commandment to 10th commandment) defines our relationship with our neighbors or our love for our neighbors. God in Leviticus 19:18 commands the Israelites: "You shall not take vengeance or bear any grudge against the sons of your own people, but you shall love your neighbor as yourself: I am the Lord." "Love your neighbor as yourself" becomes a central theme of the New Testament (Matthew 5:43, 22:39) and is expanded by including "But I say to you, 'Love your enemies and pray for those who persecute you.'" (Matthew 5:44). "Love your neighbor" is an essence for us to establish a good ethical relationship with our neighbors.

### 2. Sellers-Buyers Relation

As a seller, a Christian should be honest, using a just or accurate scale/measuring tool. Some sellers try to use dishonest scales, deceive their customers to make more immediate profit. However, in the long run, buyers will recognize the sellers' dishonesty. Proverbs 11:1 states: "A false balance is an abomination to the Lord, but a just weight is his delight," and Proverbs 20:23 states: "Diverse weights are an abomination to the Lord, and false scales are not good." Most people are both sellers and buyers at the same time. People who are buyers in the product market are sellers in the labor market. People sell their labor to make money and live with the money that they earn.

### 3. Employers-Employees Relation

Deuteronomy 24:14-15 states: "[14]You shall not oppress a hired servant who is poor and needy, whether he is one of your brethren or one of the sojourners who are in your land within your towns; [15]you shall give him his hire on the day he earns it, before the sun goes down (for he is poor, and sets his heart upon it); lest he cry against you to the Lord, and it be sin in you." God in Leviticus 19:13 tells the Israelites: "You shall not oppress your neighbor or rob him. The wages of a hired servant shall not remain with you all night until the morning." God tells the employers not to hold back of a hired worker overnight, knowing that they need daily bread. Some employers exploit their employees, paying less than the minimum wage with a delayed payment. There are some giant companies who pay late to small companies when they have contracts or subcontracts with them. Sometimes, they issue 90-day, 120-day, or even late-day promissory notes although the delivery of products is done much earlier within a month. Even some Christian colleges pay their adjunct faculty's payment late, sometimes more than one month after the course is completed, which seems to be quite unethical, knowing the message of Deuteronomy 24:15 and Leviticus 19:13.

The government imposes the minimum wage to protect workers/sellers in the labor market. The current federal minimum wage is $7.25 per hour since July 2009 although some states, cities and counties have a higher minimum wage rate. Is the federal minimum wage of $7.25, which has not increased since 2009, fair to young unskilled workers today? If a person works 40 hours per week and 52 weeks per year based on the current federal minimum wage of $7.25, he/she makes about $15,000 (before tax) a year. Although the $7.25 minimum wage seems to be a little bit too low, many employers do not want to pay this minimum hourly wage to their (young) unskilled workers. Rather, they try to hire illegal workers who are willing to work even at $3-4 per hour to settle in the United States. This may be another unethical behavior of the employers. Rabbi Michael Knopf translates Leviticus 19:16 as: "Do not profit by the blood of your fellow."[62] Many economists point out that the government's price control, including the minimum wage in the labor market, gives more negative effects than positive effects. Yet, the Bible tells us that rich people should remember their poor neighbors and should be ready to share their plenty with them.

Paul's advice for masters and servants or slaves may be applicable to employers and employees in today's society. Paul in Ephesians 6:5 and 9 states: "[5]Slaves, be obedient to those who are your earthly masters, with fear and trembling, in singleness of heart, as to Christ; ... [9]Masters, do the same to them, and forbear threatening, knowing that he who is both their Master and yours is in heaven, and that there is no partiality with him." Paul in Colossians 3:22 and 4:1 states: "[3:22]Slaves, obey in everything those who are your earthly masters, not with eyeservice, as men-pleasers, but in singleness of heart, fearing the Lord. … [4:1]Masters, treat your slaves justly and fairly, knowing that you also have a Master in heaven." When people live in this world, there are discriminations due to different races, sexes, educations, classes or ethnic backgrounds, etc. Paul, however, advises them to do their best under the given situations, Jews or Gentiles, men or women, masters or slaves/servants. Paul considered the slave system or the masters-slaves relationship as a temporary situation or environment while people lived in the world in his time.[63] The same Paul in Galatians 3:28 claims: "There is neither Jew nor Gentile, neither slave nor free, nor is there male and female, for you are all one in Christ Jesus." Paul tells us that when faith came (Galatians 3:25), we are no longer under a custodian but all children of God in Christ Jesus (3:26), and thus there is no distinction, but we are

---

[62] Michael Knopf, "A Biblical Case for Raising the Minimum Wage," *Huffington Post* (February 18, 2014). Retrieved from https://www.huffingtonpost.com/rabbi-michael-knopf/a-biblical-case-for-raisi_b_4804908.html

[63] K. P. Choi, *To Me, To Live Is Christ: Oikonomia Bible Interpretation Series 2 - Ephesians-Philippians* (in Korean). Seoul, Korea: Qumran Publishing House, 1999, 178-181.

all one in Christ Jesus (3:28). So, each of Christians should respect each other.[64]

## National Ethics in the Bible

Paul in Romans 13:1 and 6-7 states: "[1]Let every person be subject to the governing authorities. For there is no authority except from God, and those that exist have been instituted by God. … [6]For the same reason you also pay taxes, for the authorities are ministers of God, attending to this very thing. [7]Pay all of them their dues, taxes to whom taxes are due, revenue to whom revenue is due, respect to whom respect is due, honor to whom honor is due." Acknowledging that the authority of the government is from God, people should respect its authority as they revere God.[65] People should observe their duties as the citizens of the nation. The 'authority' in Greek is ἐξουσία (*exousia*), which is a compound word of ἐξ (out from) and ουσία (being, substance, or essence). Thus, an authority is given from the substance or essence – God. Paul regards the authorities of a nation or leaders are from God, and thus the leaders had not only the authorities but also the duties to God. The government or leader should govern the nation and its people according to the will of God who gives the authority. In this sense, the government or the leader is a vicar of God, who should exercise the economy of God on behalf of him. If the leader does not govern the nation and its people well, he/she is not against his people but against God who has given him/her the authority.

[64] K. P. Choi, *No Other Gospels: Oikonomia Bible Interpretation Series 4 – Galatians* (in Korean). Seoul, Korea: Qumran Publishing House, 2000, 196.

[65] K. P. Choi, *Present Your Bodies as a Living Sacrifice: Oikonomia Bible Interpretation Series 1 – Romans* (in Korean). Seoul, Korea: Qumran Publishing House, 1999, 254-257.

Chapter Twenty-Three

# Christian Ethics in Capitalism

## Private Ownership

Private ownership is a primary and typical characteristic of capitalism, which is different from government ownership in socialism and common ownership by workers in communism. In socialism all properties are owned by the government or the central authority and in communism by all workers, common ownership.

Private ownership was granted in the Old Testament, although people's ownership was entrusted or delegated, and the original ownership belonged to God, as we discussed previously. Private ownership continued in the New Testament. In the early church, Christians lived together in a community and they brought their possessions to the community as in Acts 2:43-47 and Acts 4:32-35. Although the early Christians did not claim their private ownership in this commonism, they did not deny their private ownership. That is, the early Christian community's economic system, commonism, is within the boundary of capitalism.

## Decentralized Decision Making in Markets

Another important characteristic of capitalism is decentralized decision making in the markets. It is not the central authority but the market that determines price and quantity of a good or service. The Bible does not deny markets and their functions. Sellers sell their commodities and buyers purchase them in markets.

## Business Motives in Capitalism

Producers or sellers want to maximize their profit whereas buyers want to maximize their utility – satisfaction or happiness. When a seller is too greedy to consider other people, he/she may do unethical things – lying, cheating, fraud, etc. – and even illegal activities. Recently business people have been paying more attention to environmental issues - global warming, pollution reduction, green energy, etc. - and social responsibility. Considering not only profit but also people and planet, a triple-bottom-line outcome may be a good way to do business that is beneficial not only to themselves - companies and their employees - but also to society and other members of society and to environments. As global warming is becoming a serious issue, a firm's goal that includes avoiding damages to environment by reducing emissions/negative externalities becomes more desirable.

## Ethical Issues in Capitalism

The most significant issue in capitalism is inequality. Wealth is not equally distributed, and income is not equal. Capitalism encourages people to compete each other. Some people make more money than others, and it creates income or wealth inequality. To make more money than others, some people may be tempted to cheat or do some other illegal activities. Less skilled, talented, and/or educated people have hard time to catch up more skilled, talented, and/or educated people. They find sooner or later that their wealth is much less than the others.

Greed is a part of human natures. Capitalism encourages people's greed. Moderate greed may be okay for the economy to grow, however too much greed destroys relationships among companies, people in the society. Too much greed makes people dishonest and deceive others or make ill use of others. Capitalism also causes environmental problems when firms overproduce goods and services without considering environments. Today's society experience global warming problems that are caused by chemical emissions or pollution.

## Christian Ethics in Capitalism

God does not reject capitalism although all things belong to God. However, God wants his people to use their wealth according to God's will. The richer people share their wealth with the poorer people. God's provision in the Bible is to let people offer tithes. Tithes were used not only for the Levites who were not given portions but also for the poor widows, orphans, and strangers. In today's society, the government can do the function by collecting more taxes from the rich. The government should make a whole effort to reduce income or wealth inequality by redistributing income. In this sense, it may not be pure capitalistic but a little bit socialistic attempt.

Capitalism is closely connected with a market economy in which prices and production of goods and services are determined by the interaction of supply and demand. God wants merchants or sellers to be honest and fair, not deceiving about their scales and products. Employers should not exploit their employees, knowing their needs.

In capitalism, money or wealth is too much emphasized or too much valued. It becomes an idol to many people, replacing God. That is why Jesus tells his disciples and us that we cannot serve both God and Mammon (or Money) (Matthew 6:24). And Paul says that the love of money is a root of all kinds of evil (1 Timothy 6:10). However, most people cannot deny that they love (or like) money. What Jesus and Paul meant is priority. When you love money more than God, you will be in trouble in a capitalist society. Because of your too much love of money, you may get involved in dishonest, unethical, or unlawful events.

As Edd Noell points out, capitalism is compatible with Christian ethics. [66] However, for Christian ethics to be valid in capitalism, Christians should have a right priority. That is, God should be first before anything else. Christians should be honest, diligent, not too greedy, and love their neighbors. When we love our neighbors, we will not deceive them and cheat on them.

---

[66] Noell, E. (2016). "Capitalism and Christian Ethics." *Free Market Forum* by Hillsdale College. Retrieved from https://www.hillsdale.edu/wp-content/uploads/2016/02/FMF-2013-Capitalism-and-Christian-Ethics.pdf

# EPILOGUE

## Chapter Twenty-Four

## Restoration of the Lost Paradise

In economics, when an economy is away from the full employment level, some economists (classical economists and their followers) claim that the economy has self-correcting ability whereas some other economists (Keynesian economists and their followers) claim that the government should actively implement fiscal policy and/or monetary policy to let the economy move closer to full employment.

### The Garden of Eden

Without God's intervention, can people or the government restore the lost paradise? Or can they make this world a paradise where "justice rolls down like waters, and righteousness like an everflowing stream" (Amos 5:24)? What or where is the paradise? In the Bible, God established the garden of Eden to place the first human beings there. Why was the garden of Eden so important? It was because the garden of Eden was a place where Adam and Even resided with God's blessings. In the garden of Eden, people would not have lacked anything. People would not have worried about the scarcity of resources.

### The Land of Canaan

Even after Adam and Eve fell, God could not give up human beings who were created according to his image and his likeness. God chose his people selectively – Enoch, Noah, Abraham and his descendants – to walk with them and bestow his blessings upon them. God had a plan to build another paradise in the land of Canaan. God told Abraham that he would give the land of Canaan to (him and) his descendants (Genesis 12:7, 13:15, 15:7, 15:18, 17:8, 24:7). God promised Moses and the Israelites that he would lead them to the land flowing with milk and honey (Exodus 3:8; Deuteronomy 31:20). What qualifies a paradise? The most important qualification of a paradise is God's dominion or sovereignty – God's governing activities directly or indirectly over his people.

The land of Canaan itself was not fertile. However, when God was with his people, the land would become a fertile and blessed land. God commanded the Israelites to drive out all the residents from the land of Canaan to establish his kingdom on earth. But the Israelites did not follow God's command but got along with them. The Israelites failed God's plan due to their disobedience although God still walked with his people – Gideon, Samuel, David, young Solomon, and some other kings of the Southern Kingdom after Solomon. God still wanted to build his kingdom on the earth, New Jerusalem, using his people after he let them return from Babylon. The Israelites rarely changed even after the 70-year Babylon captivity.

## The New Heaven and The New Earth

God foretold about the new heaven(s) and the new earth, another expression of the paradise, through his prophets that he would establish when an opportune time would come (Isaiah 65:17-25). God would reign here in the new heavens and the new earth. God in Isaiah 65:17-19 says: "[17]For behold, I create new heavens and a new earth; and the former things shall not be remembered or come into mind. [18]But be glad and rejoice forever in that which I create; for behold, I create Jerusalem a rejoicing, and her people a joy. [19]I will rejoice in Jerusalem and be glad in my people; no more shall be heard in it the sound of weeping and the cry of distress." Peter in 2 Peter 3:13 states: "But in keeping with his promise we are looking forward to a new heaven and a new earth, where righteousness dwells." These new heaven(s) and the new earth is the restored paradise and the kingdom of God where God is with his people. Peter explains these new heaven(s) and the new earth will be realized on the day of the Lord. John in Revelation 21:1-2 says: "[1]Then I saw a new heaven and a new earth; for the first heaven and the first earth had passed away, and the sea was no more. [2]And I saw the holy city, new Jerusalem, coming down out of heaven from God, prepared as a bride adorned for her husband"; and in Revelation 22:1-2 describes the scene of the new earth: "[1]Then he(=the angel) showed me the river of the water of life, bright as crystal, flowing from the throne of God and of the Lamb [2]through the middle of the street of the city; also, on either side of the river, the tree of life with its twelve kinds of fruit, yielding its fruit each month; and the leaves of the tree were for the healing of the nations." This scene is similar to that of the paradise where God had placed Adam and Eve. The tree of life was in the middle of the garden along with the tree of the knowledge of good and evil (Genesis 2:9). Genesis 2:9b states: "In the middle of the garden were the tree of life and the tree of the knowledge of good and evil" (NIV). Adam and Eve could have lived forever if they had eaten the fruit from the tree of life instead of the fruit from the tree of the knowledge of good and evil. When Adam and Eve fell, God hid the tree of life to forbid them to eat the fruit from the tree of life and live forever (Genesis 3:22). However, the tree of life is there in the new Jerusalem, the new heaven and the new earth.

John in Revelation 22:17 states: "The Spirit and the bride say, 'Come!' And let the one who hears say, 'Come!' Let the one who is thirsty come; and let the one who wishes take the free gift of the water of life." This invitation to the water of life is similar to God's invitation to the waters in Isaiah 55:1: "Come, all you who are thirsty, come to the waters; and you who have no money, come, buy and eat! Come, buy wine and milk without money and without cost." God's invitation or calling of people to the water of life that began in the Old Testament will be completed when the new heaven and the new earth arrive. Then, the economy of God will also be fully realized.

## Restoration of the Lost Paradise Today

How long should we wait until we see the restored paradise? The lost paradise will be restored on the day of the Lord, that is, when the Lord Jesus returns to us. However, the kingdom of God – the paradise – can be realized in our life even today when we acknowledge the sovereignty of God. Jesus in Luke 17:20-21 tells his disciples: "[20]Being asked by the Pharisees when the kingdom of God was coming, he answered them, "The kingdom of God is not coming with signs to be observed; [21]nor will they say, 'Lo, here it is!' or 'There!' for behold, the kingdom of God is in the midst of you." The New Living Translation (NLT) translates Verse 21b as "For the kingdom of God is already among you." What Jesus meant here is not denying the actual kingdom of God would not come but explaining how the kingdom of God would be like. Jesus in the following verses tells about the coming of the kingdom of God: "The days are coming when you will desire to see one of the days of the Son of man, and you will not see it" (Luke 17:22). When we live by the Word of God, the kingdom of God – the new heaven and the new earth, the paradise – will be realized in our life today although we, along with all other creatures, are eagerly waiting for the returning Lord (Romans 8:18-25).

According to Paul, not only God's people but also all other creatures are waiting for the coming of God's kingdom as they were unwillingly subjected to God's curse when Adam and Eve fell but hope that they will join God's people in glorious freedom from its bondage to decay (Romans 8:19-21). John closes the book of Revelation with his wish and prayer, in Revelation 22:20-21: "[20]He who testifies to these things says, 'Surely I am coming soon.' Amen. Come, Lord Jesus! (ἔρχου κύριε Ἰησοῦ; מרנא תא, marana tha). [21]The grace of the Lord Jesus be with all the saints. Amen." When the kingdom of God comes, the economy of God – God's governing activities will be there for us.

APPENDIX

# Names/Characteristics of God

## Jehovah Compounds

Jehovah (יְהוָה = YHWH, …., tetragrammaton: I Am That I Am, Self-existent God, Exodus 3:14, 6:2-4, 34:5-7; Psalms 102)

Jehovah-Bore (The LORD Creator, Genesis 1:1, Job 38:1-41, 39:1-30, 40:1; Psalm 33:6; Isaiah 40:28-31)

Jehovah-Eloheikhem (The LORD your God, Leviticus 19:3, 4)

Jehovah-Gmolah (The LORD of recompense, Jeremiah 51:56)

Jehovah-Ishmilkjama (Jehovah is man of war, Exodus 15:3)

Jehovah-Jireh (The LORD who provides or sees, Genesis 22:14)

Jehovah-Kjacac (Jehovah is our ruler, Isaiah 33:22)

Jehovah-Kjail (The LORD is my strength, Exodus 15:2; Habakkuk 3:19)

Jehovah-Magen (The LORD is my shield, Genesis 15:1, Psalm 91:4)

Jehovah-Makjse (The LORD is my hope, Job 11:18; Psalms 14:6, 39:7, 71:5, 91:2, 91:9, 121; Joel 3:16)

Jehovah-Melek (The LORD is our King, 1 Samuel 12:12; Isaiah 33:22)

Jehovah-M'kaddesh, Jehovah-Mekoddishkem (The LORD who sanctifies you, Exodus 31:12-13; Leviticus 20:8, 21:8, 22:32; Ezekiel 20:12)

Jehovah-Nakah (The LORD who smites, Ezekiel 7:9)

Jehovah-Nissi (The LORD is my banner or miracle, Exodus 17:15; Deuteronomy 20:3-4; Isaiah 11:10-12)

Jehovah-Osenu or Jehovah-O'saynu (The LORD our maker, Psalm 95:6)

Jehovah-Rapha or Jehovah-Rophekha (The LORD who heals you, Exodus 15:25-27; Psalms 103:3, 147:3)

Jehovah-Roi or Jehova-Raah (The LORD is my shepherd, Psalms 23:1; Isaiah 53:6, Ezekiel 34:2)

Jehoah-Sali or Jehvah-Selah (The LORD is my rock, Psalm 18:2)

Jehovah-Shalom (The LORD is peace, Numbers 6:26; Judges 6:24; Isaiah 9:6)

Jehovah-Shammah (The LORD is there, Ezekiel 48:35, Psalm 46)

Jehovah-Shafat (The LORD is our judge, Isaiah 33:22)

Jehovah-Tsevaot or Jehovah-Sabaoth (The LORD of hosts, 1 Samuel 1:3, 17:45; Psalms 46:7; Malachi 1:10-14)

Jehovah-Tsidkenu (The LORD is our righteousness, Jeremiah 23:6, 33:16)

Jehovah-Tsuri ve goali (The LORD is my Rock and my Redeemer, Psalm 19:14)

## El Constructs

Elohim (The almighty God, the triune God, Genesis 1:1-3; Deuteronomy 10:17; Psalms 68)

Elohim-Chaiyim (The living God, Jeremiah 10:10)

Elohim-Kedoshim (Our holy God, Leviticus 19:2; Joshua 24:19)

El-Chaiyai (The God of my life, Psalm 42:8)

El-Channum (The gracious God, Jonah 4:2)

El-Chuwl (The God who gave you life, Isaiah 43:1-3; Psalm 139:13-18)

E-De'ot, El-Deah (The God of knowledge, 1 Samuelson 2:3)

El-Echad (The One God, Malachi 2:10)

El-Elohe Israel (The mighty God of Israel, Genesis 33:20; Exodus 5:1; Psalms 68:8, 106:48)

El-Elyon (The most high God, Genesis 14:20, 22; Numbers 24:16; Psalm 7:17, 9:2, 47:2; Daniel 4:34)

El-Emeth (The God of truth, Psalm 31:5)

El-Emunah (The faithful God, Deuteronomy 32:4)

El-Gibbor (The mighty God, Isaiah 9:6)

El-Hagadol (The great God, Deuteronomy 10:17)

El-Hakavod (The God of glory, Psalm 29:3)

El-Hakkadosh (The holy God, the holy One, Isaiah 5:16)

E-Hanne'eman (The faithful God, Deuteronomy 7:9)

El-Hannora (The awesome God, Nehemiah 9:32)

El-Hashamyim (The God of the heavens, Psalm 136:26)

El-Israel (The God of Israel, Psalm 68:36)

El-Olam (The everlasting God, Genesis 21:33; Psalms 90:1-2, 93:2; Isaiah 26:4, 40:28)

El-Kanna or El-Kanno (The jealous God, Exodus 20:5, 34:14; Numbers 5:14, 30; Deuteronomy 4:24, 5:9, 6:15; Joshua 24:19)

El-Rachum (The God of mercy or compassion, Deuteronomy 4:31)

El-Roi (The God who sees, Genesis 16:13; Psalms 139:7-12)

El-Sali (The God of my strength or my rock, Psalm 42:9)

El-Shaddai (The almighty or all-sufficient God, Genesis 17:1, 28:3, 35:11, 43:14, 48:3, 49:25; Exodus 6:3; Numbers 24:6; Ruth 1:20; Psalms 22:10, 68:15, 91:1; Ezekiel 1:24, 10:25, 23:21)

El-Simchat Gili (The God of the joy of my exaltation, Psalm 43:4)

El-Tzadik (The righteous God, Isaiah 45:21), 26; Isaiah 44:2)

El-Yeshuati (The God of my salvation, Isaiah 12:2)

El-Yeshuatenu (The God of our salvation, Psalm 68:19)

El-Yeshurun (The God of Jeshurun – "the righteous people", Deuteronomy 32:15, 33:5)

Immanuel (God is with us, Isaiah 7:14)

Elohay Chasdi (God of my kindness, Psalm 59:11-18)

Elohay Elohim (God of gods, Deuteronomy 10:17)

Elohay Kedem (God of the beginning, Deuteronomy 33:27)

Elohay Marom (God of heights, Micah 6:6)

Elohay Mauzi (God of my strength, Psalm 43:2)

Elohay Mikarov (God who is near, Jeremiah 23:23)

Elohay Selichot (God of forgiveness, Nehemiah 9:17)

Elohay Tehilati (God of my praise, Psalm 109:1)

Elohay Yishi (God of my salvation, Psalms 18:47, 25:5)

**Sources**

https://www.bibliatodo.com/en/names-of-God

https://www.hebrew4christians.com/Names_of_G-d/El/el.html

https://www.hebrew4christians.com/Names_of_G-d/YHVH/yhvh.html

# BIBLIOGRAPHY

## English Bible Versions Used

| | |
|---|---|
| **RSV** | **Revised Standard Version (Primary)** |
| CEB | Common English Bible |
| ESV | English Standard Version |
| GNT | Good News Translation |
| ISV | International Standard Version |
| KJV | King James Version |
| NIV | New International Version |
| NLT | New Living Translation |
| NRSV | New Revised Standard Version |
| TLB | The Living Bible |

## Books

Barrett, C. K. *A Commentary on the Second Epistle to the Corinthians.* Harper & Row, 1973.

Barringer, B. R. and Ireland, R. D. *Entrepreneurship: Successfully Launching New Ventures* (4th ed.), Pearson, 2011.

Choi, K. P. *Paul's Life, Epistles, and the Central Themes of His Theology* (in Korean). Seoul, Korea: Qumran Publishing House, 2013.

________. *No Other Gospel: Oikonomia Bible Interpretation Series 6 – Galatians* (in Korean). Seoul, Korea: Qumran Publishing House, 2005.

________. *When I Am Weak, Then I Am Strong: Oikonomia Bible Interpretation Series 5 – 2 Corinthians* (in Korean). Seoul, Korea: Qumran Publishing House, 2001.

________. *Except Jesus Christ and Him Crucified: Oikonomia Bible Interpretation Series 4 – 1 Corinthians* (in Korean). Seoul, Korea: Qumran Publishing House, 2000.

________. *For To Me, To Live Is Christ: Oikonomia Bible Interpretation Series 2 – Ephesians-Philippians* (in Korean). Seoul, Korea: Qumran Publishing House, 1999.

________. *Present Your Bodies as a Living Sacrifice: Oikonomia Bible Interpretation Series 1 – Romans* (in Korean). Seoul, Korea: Qumran Publishing House, 1999.

Claar, V. V. and Klay, R. J. *Economics in Christian Perspective: Theory, Policy and Life Choices*, Downers Grove, IL: IVP Press, 2007.

Dayton, H. *Your Money Counts.* Carol Stream, IL: Tyndale House Publishers, Inc., 1996.

Endo, S. *Silence.* Picador Modern Classics, 2016.

Eusebius Pamphilus. *The Ecclesiastical History.* (trans.) C. F. Cruse, Grand Rapids, MI: Baker Boon House, 1993.

Ferrell, O. C., Fraedrich, J., and Ferrell, L. *Business Ethics: Ethical Decision Making and Cases* (12th ed.). Cengage Learning, 2019 (2017).

Meeks, M. D. *God the Economist.* Minneapolis, Minnesota: Fortress Press, 1973 (1946).

Nickle, K. F. *The Collection: A Study in Paul's Strategy.* Alec R. Allenson Inc., 1966.

Thayer, J. *Greek-English Lexicon of the New Testament.* Grand Rapids, MI: Zondervan Publishing House, 1978.

Tucker, I. B. *Economics for Today* (10th ed.). Boston, MA: Cengage Learning, 2019.

Witham, L. Marketplace of the Gods: How Economics Explain Religion. New York, NY: Oxford University Press, 2010.

**Articles**

Anderson, T. M. and Maibom, J. "The Trade-Off between Efficiency and Equity." VOX (May 29, 2016). Retrieved from https://voxeu.org/article/trade-between-efficiency-and-equity

Anonymous. "Communism vs. Socialism." *Diffen* (n.d.). Retrieved from https://www.diffen.com/difference/Communism_vs_Socialism

ATS Bible Dictionary. "Market." *BibleHub* (n.d.) Retrieved from https://biblehub.com/topical/m/market.htm

Bob Becking, "Biblical Games: Game Theory and the Hebrew Bible," *Ars Disputandi*, Vol. 3, 2003, 91-93

Buck, J. "Economic Efficiency and Equity." *Economic Perspectives* (February 10, 208). Retrieved from http://econperspectives.blogspot.com/2008/02/economic-efficiency-and-equity.html

Elawart, S. "Biblical Principles of Economics." *Koinonia House* (October 1, 2011). Retrieved from https://www.khouse.org/articles/2011/1015/

Foerster. "χάρις." Theological Dictionary of the New Testament, edited by G. Kittel and G. Friedrich, Vol. 9, 1974.

Hall, S. "Econ omics: Equity vs. Efficiency." *Bizfluent.* (September 26, 2017). Retrieved from https://bizfluent.com/about-7230309-economics--equity-vs--efficiency.html

Knopf, M. "A Biblical Case for Raising the Minimum Wage," *Huffington Post* (February 18, 2014). Retrieved from https://www.huffingtonpost.com/rabbi-michael-knopf/a-biblical-case-for-raisi_b_4804908.html

Munger, S. "The Bible and Food." *All About God* (n.d.). Retrieved from https://www.allaboutgod.com/the-bible-and-food.htm

Noell, E. "Capitalism and Christian Ethics." *Free Market Forum* by Hillsdale College (2016). Retrieved from https://www.hillsdale.edu/wp-content/uploads/2016/02/FMF-2013-Capitalism-and-Christian-Ethics.pdf

Rose, J. "10 Bible Verses Every Entrepreneur Needs to Read." *Good Financial Cents* (August 12, 2013). Retrieved from https://www.goodfinancialcents.com/bible-verses-about-business-entrepreneurship

Strong's Hebrew Concordance. "1431. gadal." *BibleHub* (n.d.) Retrieved from https://biblehub.com/hebrew/1431.htm

____________. "2428. chayil." *BibleHub* (n.d.) Retrieved from https://biblehub.com/hebrew/2428.htm

____________. "2610. chaneph." *BibleHub* (n.d.) Retrieved from https://biblehub.com/hebrew/2610.htm

____________. "3384. yarah or yara." *BibleHub* (n.d.) Retrieved from https://biblehub.com/hebrew/3384.htm

____________. "4043. magen or meginnah." *BibleHub* (n.d.) Retrieved from https://biblehub.com/hebrew/4043.htm

____________. "4268. machaseh or machseh." *BibleHub* (n.d.) Retrieved from https://biblehub.com/hebrew/4268.htm

____________. "4339. meshar." *BibleHub* (n.d.) Retrieved from https://biblehub.com/hebrew/4339.htm

_____________. "4399. melakah." *BibleHub* (n.d.) Retrieved from https://biblehub.com/hebrew/4399.htm

_____________. "4627. maarab." *BibleHub* (n.d.) Retrieved from https://biblehub.com/hebrew/4627.htm

_____________. "4686. matsuwd." *BibleHub* (n.d.) Retrieved from https://biblehub.com/hebrew/4686.htm

_____________. "4869. misgab." *BibleHub* (n.d.) Retrieved from https://biblehub.com/hebrew/4869.htm

_____________. "4943. mesheq." *BibleHub* (n.d.) Retrieved from https://biblehub.com/hebrew/4943.htm

_____________. "5503. sachar." *BibleHub* (n.d.) Retrieved from https://biblehub.com/hebrew/5503.htm

_____________. "5504. sachar." *BibleHub* (n.d.) Retrieved from https://biblehub.com/hebrew/5504.htm

_____________. "5505. sachar." *BibleHub* (n.d.) Retrieved from https://biblehub.com/hebrew/5505.htm

_____________. "5647. abad." *BibleHub* (n.d.) Retrieved from https://biblehub.com/hebrew/5647.htm

_____________. "6093. itstsabon." *BibleHub* (n.d.) Retrieved from https://biblehub.com/hebrew/6093.htm

_____________. "6666. tsedaqah." *BibleHub* (n.d.) Retrieved from https://biblehub.com/hebrew/6666.htm

_____________. "7235. rabah." *BibleHub* (n.d.) Retrieved from https://biblehub.com/hebrew/7235.htm

_____________. "8104. shamar." *BibleHub* (n.d.) Retrieved from https://biblehub.com/hebrew/8104.htm

Thayer's Greek Lexicon. "1577. ἐκκλησία." *BibleHub* (n.d.) Retrieved from https://biblehub.com/str/greek/1577.htm

Whelchel, H. "Three Key Passages Concerning Stewardship in the Bible." *Institute for Faith, Work, & Economics* (October 19, 2016). Retrieved from https://tifwe.org/stewardship-in-the-bible

_________. "Four Principles of Biblical Stewardship." *Institute for Faith, Work, & Economics* (November 26, 2012). Retrieved from https://tifwe.org/four-principles-of-biblical-stewardship/

www.ingramcontent.com/pod-product-compliance
Lightning Source LLC
LaVergne TN
LVHW022041200926
848481LV00003B/737
* 9 7 9 8 8 9 5 3 2 0 4 0 2 *